RORKE'S
DRIFT 1879
& ISANDLWANA

RORKE'S DRIFT 1879
& ISANDLWANA

A BATTLEFIELD GUIDE

CHRIS PEERS

First published 2017
Reprinted 2017

The History Press
The Mill, Brimscombe Port
Stroud, Gloucestershire, GL5 2QG
www.thehistorypress.co.uk

British Library Cataloguing in Publication Data.
A catalogue record for this book is available from the British Library.

ISBN 978 0 7509 6730 3

Typesetting and origination by The History Press
Printed and bound in Turkey by Imak.

Contents

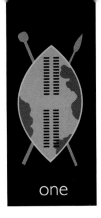

one

Introduction and Acknowledgements

At the beginning of 1879 a series of events occurred in what is now Kwazulu-Natal Province, South Africa, that shook the British Empire to its core. At that time Britain was by far the greatest of the European 'great powers' that were in the process of dividing the rest of the world among them, and as the world's leading industrial economy it could provide its armies with the very latest in military technology. Africa, on the other hand, was generally regarded as backward and unsophisticated, its warriors still relying on spears or obsolete and dilapidated muskets traded by unscrupulous arms dealers. Two of the continent's greatest kingdoms had already suffered defeat at the hands of the British – Ethiopia in 1868 and Ashanti in 1874, both of them principally because of the inability of their unquestionably courageous fighting men to stand up to British firepower in pitched battle. Within South Africa itself the Xhosa of the Eastern Cape had just lost the last of nine Cape Frontier Wars for the same reason; although the Xhosa spearmen could be deadly when fighting from ambush, their armies quickly melted away under fire from breech-loading rifles. But on 22 January 1879 a powerful British column invading Zululand was decisively defeated beneath a hill called Isandlwana – not by trickery or ambush, but in what used to be called a 'fair fight' in the open – losing nearly half its men, including a whole battalion of regular infantry virtually wiped out. Then, later on the same day, a garrison of no more than 100 British troops was attacked furiously by forty times their number of Zulus at the mission station at Rorke's Drift, only a few miles from Isandlwana. But on this occasion the British held out against all reasonable expectations, eventually beating off their attackers and winning eleven Victoria Crosses (VCs) between them – still the most VCs ever won in a single day's action. This epic story would be enough by itself to explain the enduring interest in the war, but it was the release in

The spectacular view eastwards across Zululand from the grounds of Rorke's Drift Lodge on the slopes of the Biggarsberg Mountains.

1966 of Cy Endfield and Stanley Baker's film *Zulu* that secured its place as the archetypal tale of Victorian heroism.

The two sites where these battles were fought have been places of pilgrimage ever since. Naturally they have always been especially popular with British visitors, although an increasing number are now coming from the USA and other countries. Sheer distance means that they are still a once in a lifetime trip for many enthusiasts, but they are relatively accessible, even for those with limited mobility, and a visit will often form part of a longer tour of South Africa, a country that offers a wide variety of fascinating experiences. Isandlwana and Rorke's Drift are separate battlefields, located about 14km apart, but for several reasons it makes sense to treat them together. The battles were fought on the same day, between elements of the same armies, and a few men even fought in both. It would be impossible to understand the action at Rorke's Drift without a knowledge of the events that took place a few hours earlier at Isandlwana. Visiting the sites today underlines even more emphatically the close connections between them. No one is likely to travel so far to see one of them without visiting the other less than an hour's drive away, and the tours run by both international operators and local guides are almost invariably organised on this principle. At the sites themselves there is also a considerable amount of overlap in the information on display. The memorial to the 24th Regiment of Foot at Isandlwana, for example, commemorates the dead of both battles, and the visitor centre there features one of the most comprehensive rolls of the defenders of Rorke's Drift. Conversely, the easiest way to understand the effects of the terrain at Isandlwana is to examine the excellent three-dimensional terrain model at the Rorke's Drift museum.

Both sites have been affected by modern development, but from a visitor's point of view they have if anything been enhanced rather than damaged: the buildings at Rorke's Drift, for example, post-date the battle, but have been built on the same foundations as the originals and in a very similar style. The surrounding countryside is just untamed enough to give a flavour of Africa, but there are now luxury lodges within easy reach. Coach tours starting in Durban or Johannesburg regularly bring parties from further afield. Nevertheless, the battlefields are seldom overcrowded, except perhaps when special events are organised, and independent travellers will often have the sites almost to themselves.

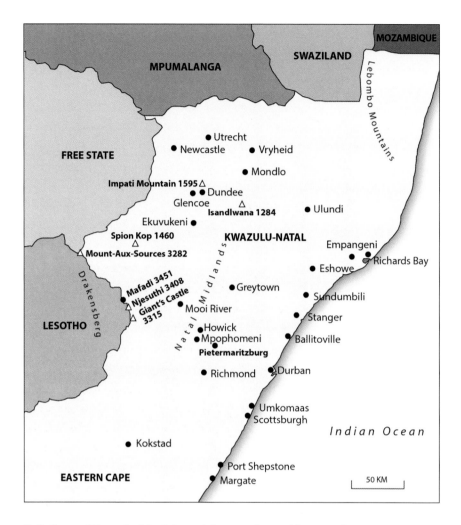

Relief map of Kwazulu-Natal. (copyright www.freeworldmaps.net)

The aim of this guide is to assist the visitor to these two sites with details on how to get there, where to stay, and how to make sense of the events that happened there nearly 140 years ago. The principal source of information is the author's visit in October 2015. Many people will prefer to go on an organised tour, with professional guides included, an option that will take a lot of the work out of planning a trip. For those who are on a tighter budget, or simply prefer to travel independently, it is perfectly possible to do so, and they should find all the information they need here. It is also to be hoped that the up-to-date overview of the current condition of the battlefields may be of interest to those who are not currently planning a visit, or have done so in the past.

In order to get the best out of a tour it is necessary to understand at least the general outline of what was a very complicated – and still controversial – sequence of events. In the case of both battles there are a handful of accounts from the Zulu side, but these come only from junior officers or rank and file warriors, so while they can shed very useful light on particular events we have next to no information on the Zulu battle plans.

The great majority of the British participants at Isandlwana were killed there, including both colonels, and all the officers and men of the regular infantry companies, while those men who survived escaped before the final phase of the battle. Therefore, many of the events surrounding it have to be pieced together from fragmentary and sometimes contradictory accounts. These can be supplemented by battlefield archaeology and what is known as 'inherent military probability', which basically involves asking 'what would – or should – professional soldiers have done in this situation?' Several modern accounts have done an excellent job of this, but the fact remains that we know less than we would like to about what actually happened. Of course, because this was a disaster for the British Army, there has also been a long-running controversy about who was to blame. I have tried on the whole to steer clear of this, having much sympathy for the view that it is more constructive to look at it not as a British defeat but as a Zulu victory. Rorke's Drift, on the other hand, is very well documented, at least from the British side. We have several detailed accounts from participants, including the report of the officer commanding, Lieutenant Chard, and another from an experienced senior non-commissioned officer (NCO), Colour Sergeant Bourne. The names of the combatants (with a few minor uncertainties), the casualties and even the nature of their wounds are recorded, while in some cases we are given, or can reconstruct with varying degrees of certainty, the precise movements of individuals during the battle. But even here we can hardly expect the survivors to have kept a detailed record of events as they were happening, and the inevitable confusion of battle is reflected in their various accounts.

I offer the version given here not as an expert on the Anglo-Zulu War, but merely as someone with a little knowledge of nineteenth-century African warfare who has seen the battlefields with what he hopes is a fresh eye. It is not the intention to go into great detail about every phase of the fighting, as the historical events have already been very well covered in numerous books, a selection of which are listed on pages 184–87. My brief account of the battles is intended purely to explain something of the background to the non-expert visitor. It is based almost entirely on secondary sources and information supplied by the people mentioned below, supplemented by personal impressions of the terrain, and has no real pretensions to scholarship. Inevitably it will reflect a personal opinion on some questions that are still debated, but those who want to examine the issues in depth should consult the works of the experts. Those individuals credited here have provided many insights that I have found very valuable, but they can in no way be held responsible for any errors, omissions or misinterpretations on my part.

Among the many people who have helped with the research for this guide, I would particularly like to thank the following:

Paul and Christine Lamberth and the staff at Rorke's Drift Lodge. Thanks to Paul's vast knowledge of the area and its history I have been able to visit places I would otherwise not have seen, and to understand much more clearly what I was seeing. I can recommend him very highly as a guide.

Thulani Khuzwayo at Rorke's Drift. Thulani has been extremely generous with his time, and in conversations with him I have gained new perspectives on the Zulu view of their own history as well as on events in present-day South Africa.

Ray Boyles, for the loan of books, CDs and photographs from sites I have not managed to visit, as well as for his extensive list of useful contacts.

Alan Rogers and John Peers, for trusting me with their photographic equipment.

And not least my wife Kate and my children Megan and John, for patiently putting up with me disappearing to the other side of the world and pretending it was all 'work'.

A note on measurements and distances: South Africa today uses the metric system, but Lord Chelmsford's army used imperial feet, yards and miles, or more informally paces – a system with which many older British people are still more familiar. For most purposes, such as distances when travelling by road, I have adopted the metric measurements that the visitor will encounter on road signs and other local sources of information, but where a mention of distances on the battlefields is derived from a nineteenth-century source I have left it in its original form.

The landscape of northern Zululand, looking south-west from the St Lucia–Hlobane road in the direction of Ulundi. Even today the contrast is marked between the more enclosed and wooded countryside of Natal south of the Buffalo and Tugela rivers, with its fenced farms, sugarcane fields and eucalyptus plantations, and the wide horizons of Zululand proper.

LANGUAGES

South Africa has eleven official languages – more than any other country in the world – but English is the most widely spoken, and the only one that you are likely to need. The most commonly encountered local idiom is 'braai', which is a barbecue, but if you have to ask directions anywhere, also remember that a 'robot' is a traffic light. Place names in Kwazulu-Natal may be derived from English, Afrikaans or isiZulu, as the Zulu language is properly known. In the nineteenth century isiZulu was not a written language, and British writers rendered local words and place names in a bewildering variety of ways. Isandlwana, for example, appears in different sources as Isandhlwana, Insalwana or even Isandula. I have tried to give these words in the form which the battlefield visitor is most likely to encounter today, but there will inevitably be a few inconsistencies. Names, especially those of places and military units, often begin with a prefix before the noun, which is written with a lower case initial letter: for example the language *isiZulu* or the uKhandempemvu Regiment. However, well-known places are usually rendered in English in a more familiar form, hence you will see Kwazulu rather than kwa-Zulu, and Isandlwana rather than iSandlwana, a convention that I have followed here.

The Zulu language contains a number of sounds that cannot easily be expressed in English, and which English speakers often struggle to reproduce anyway. Suffice it to say that in the modern written language the letters c, q and x represent different types of clicks, so that in the name of the town of Nqutu, for example, the 'q' is pronounced by curling back the tip of the tongue against the roof of the mouth and then flicking it forward. This seems easy enough after a few minutes' solo practice, but doing it fluently in conversation is another matter. Luckily the local people are very tolerant of outsiders' efforts, and if you end up saying something like 'Nkutu' they will still know where you mean. In fact, all Zulus of school age and above will be fluent in English, though most seem to be genuinely appreciative of efforts to address them in their own language, however haltingly. In contrast to the situation in so many places, they will not ignore your pitiful efforts or insist on speaking to you in English regardless. It is not within the scope of this book to offer lessons in isiZulu, but even a casual 'sawubona, unjani?' ('Hello, how are you?') is a good way to break the ice (the expected answer is 'ngiyaphila', 'I am fine'). 'Yebo', 'yes' or 'OK' seems to have got into the South African idiom generally, and you might hear it even in conversations carried on in English.

SHAKA ZULU

The Zulu nation was founded by King Shaka kaSenzangakhona (the prefix *ka* meaning 'son of'), who reigned from 1816 to 1828, and whose nephew Cetshwayo kaMpande was on the throne in 1879. Outside South Africa Shaka has long enjoyed a reputation as a tyrant, a monster of cruelty who murdered his own people on a whim, and whose campaigns of conquest depopulated huge areas of the interior. This is not the place for a lengthy discussion of the real nature of his rule, but the visitor may be surprised to discover that the view of Shaka prevalent in Zululand today is very different. For those arriving in Durban by air the first clue will be the name of their destination: King Shaka International Airport. From the coast road south of the town of kwaDukuza-Stanger – once the site of the king's *kraal*, or base – a sign points to Shaka's Rock, where the king is said to have sat and contemplated the sea and the invaders that it was bringing to his land. (An alternative story, more in line with the traditional 'monster' theme, has it that he threw his enemies from the rock to drown.) In the town itself a memorial marks the spot where he was assassinated. In Durban a major new attraction is uShaka Marine World, situated on King Shaka Avenue. And near Eshowe there is Shakaland, a theme park that offers reconstructions of traditional Zulu life and culture. As long ago as 1994 the king's new image was the subject of an academic book, *Inventing Shaka*, by Daphna Golan (Boulder, Colorado: Lynne Rienner Publishers, 1994), and since then the process has continued. Today, the visitor might well find it hard to discover anyone in Kwazulu-Natal, black or white, who has a bad word to say about him.

Their argument is that the stories of his cruelty were invented or exaggerated by the white traders who wrote about him in order to emphasise their own courage and sell their books, and certainly many of them are old chestnuts, told about countless tyrants throughout history. The undoubted tragedy that the wars of his reign involved for large areas of southern Africa could be seen as an unintended consequence of Zulu success in what were essentially defensive campaigns, and in any case the devastation might have been exaggerated by white men who took advantage of the chaos to seize land. On the other hand, Shaka undoubtedly founded a great nation – admittedly by violent means, but that was hardly unusual in that time and place – and showed himself to be an outstanding military innovator. He was forward thinking in his attitude to European inventions and was interested in such unlikely subjects as the migration of birds. It is even possible that his notorious disapproval of marriage and sexual activity was prompted by a realisation that overpopulation was driving much of the unrest in the region. It is difficult to untangle the reality from the conflicting traditions, and much of what we think we know about Shaka's life might be mythical in any case, but it is obvious that as a symbol of local pride he continues to extend his influence well beyond the Zulu people themselves.

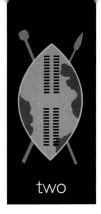

two

Background to the Anglo-Zulu War

A detailed account of the causes as well as the conduct of the war is beyond the scope of this guide. The visitor to this rather remote corner of Africa might, however, be excused for wondering what the British Army was doing there in the first place, and what threat the Zulus could possibly have posed to warrant the deployment of a full-scale expeditionary force so far from home. The ultimate cause of the war was that the Zulus – whether they knew it or not – occupied a strategic position on the sea route to India. India was by far the most important of Britain's overseas possessions, and the source of immense wealth for its traders and investors. The main reason for the British occupation of Cape Town in 1806 was its value as a supply base and naval port on the sea route to India around the Cape of Good Hope. Unlike most of the continent, the southern tip of Africa proved inviting to white settlers – both the Boers, descendants of the Dutch farmers who had arrived in the seventeenth century, and the more recent British immigrants – and the authorities at the Cape were gradually forced to extend their power inland to protect and control them. In the 1830s many Boers trekked north in the hope of escaping British control, eventually establishing independent republics in the Orange Free State and the Transvaal. Meanwhile, the British founded what was to become the city of Durban on the east coast, in a region that earlier Portuguese explorers had christened Natal.

The Natal colony was well beyond the imperial frontier at that time, and the settlers' claim to the area was based on an award by Shaka, the ruler of the neighbouring Zulu kingdom, who in 1824 had granted permission for a small colony of traders to establish themselves there. This Zulu kingdom was a very different sort of political entity from most of those encountered by white settlers elsewhere in sub-Saharan Africa. Its role in the history of the region was so dominant that it is easy to forget that in 1879 it had only been in existence for around sixty years. The Zulus were a branch of the Nguni people, descendants of the Bantu from the north who had brought their cattle to graze on the rich grasslands of what is now Kwazulu-Natal hundreds of years before. Cattle, in fact, were fundamental to Zulu culture and society, and remain so to this day. In the eighteenth century the tribes living north of the Thukela (or Tugela) River and east of the Drakensberg Mountains had been grouped into four main clans: the Ngwame, Mthethwa, Ndwandwe and Qwabe. As their population grew and grazing land became scarcer, a series of increasingly bitter wars broke out between the rival clans. At first these were fought in the traditional style, which mainly involved hurling insults and spears from a distance, a practice known as *giya*. But around 1816 a young soldier of fortune named Shaka, who had formerly been in the service of the Mthethwa chief Dingiswayo, seized power among a small sub-clan called the *amaZulu* or Zulus, the 'people of heaven', and revolutionised their tiny army with a series of military reforms. The throwing spears were abandoned and replaced by the famous short stabbing assegai, or *iklwa*; shields became larger, and the Zulus were instructed to abandon their indecisive skirmishing tactics and instead to charge their opponents and kill them in hand-to-hand combat.

Historians still debate the question of whether Shaka actually invented the new weapons and tactics or merely popularised them, but either way there can be no doubt of their effectiveness. Over the next decade he destroyed one rival army after another, incorporating many of the defeated into the rapidly growing Zulu kingdom, while sending others fleeing in all directions. This upheaval affected the entire south-eastern quarter of the continent, and later became notorious as the *mfecane*, or 'crushing'. In fact, most of the Zulus' neighbours in the late nineteenth century – the Swazis to the north, the Sotho in the Drakensberg and the Matabele of what is now Zimbabwe, to name only the most prominent – were descended at least partly from these refugees. Shaka was assassinated in 1828, but the kingdom he established endured. Under his successor, Dingaan, the Zulus fought against the Boers who were trekking up from the Cape Colony, and suffered a disastrous defeat when they tried to attack a prepared wagon *laager* at Blood River in 1838. A subsequent Boer invasion force was ambushed on the White Imfolozi River and forced to retire, but the discredited Dingaan was overthrown in the following year by his half-brother, Mpande. Meanwhile, British and Boer settlers were flooding into the territory south of the Thukela River, and in 1844 Natal was officially annexed by Cape Colony.

Mpande reigned until 1872, and carefully kept the peace with his white neighbours. But in 1856 his kingdom was convulsed by a civil war between two of his sons, Mbuyazi and Cetshwayo. In December of that year the dispute was resolved in an exceptionally bloody battle at Ndondakusuka in which Cetshwayo's supporters, known as the uSuthu, slaughtered the warriors of his brother's isiGqoza faction on the banks of the Thukela. The surviving isiGqoza fled across the river into Natal, providing the nucleus for a growing community of Zulu dissidents there, but despite a number of incidents the authorities in Natal maintained peaceful relations with Cetshwayo and recognised him as king on the death of his father. Cetshwayo, on his part, still regarded the Transvaal Boers as his main external enemy, and was eager for an alliance with the British. In August 1873 Theophilus Shepstone, the Natal Secretary for Native Affairs, was actually invited to 'crown' him, but this apparently friendly initiative was to give rise to trouble in the future. It is unlikely that the Zulu king intended the coronation to signify that he needed British consent to take the throne, but Shepstone chose to interpret it that way, announcing a list of new 'laws' to which Cetshwayo was supposed to have agreed. It is likely that this was already part of a long-term strategy to undermine the Zulu kingdom. Diamonds had recently been discovered at Kimberley further west, and the prospect that southern Africa might become economically important for its own sake inspired the British to tighten their grip on the region. The buzzword at the time was 'confederation', which basically meant bringing the various territories south of the Limpopo River into a formal political alignment. As the most powerful native African state surviving in the region, Zululand could hardly have been left out of this arrangement, especially as the British authorities were anxious to conciliate the Zulus' arch enemies, the Boers.

Things began to move towards their inevitable conclusion when in 1877 Sir Bartle Frere arrived as the new High Commissioner for South Africa. Frere was a convinced imperialist, who regarded it as his duty to extend British rule over the remaining independent black nations in the region. Soon afterwards Britain annexed the Transvaal. The annexation proved to be short-lived as the Boers were soon to throw off British control in the First Anglo-Boer War of 1881, but in the meantime the British government found itself embroiled in a longstanding dispute between its new subjects and the Zulus. Over several decades Boer farmers had been encroaching into what became known as the 'disputed territory' of north-western Zululand, situated east of the Buffalo River upstream from Rorke's Drift. Cetshwayo now invited Shepstone – whom he still saw as an ally – to mediate in the dispute. In fact, Shepstone had by now become convinced (on little if any evidence) that the Zulus were a threat to the security of Natal, and furthermore in his new capacity as Administrator of the Transvaal he was anxious not to provoke the Boers into rebellion. So he advised the king to accept the Boer claim to the disputed lands. Cetshwayo naturally refused and the issue was referred to a boundary commission, which met at Rorke's Drift in March 1878. To the horror of Shepstone and Frere the commission supported the most important part of the Zulu claim, awarding the Boers only a small stretch of land between the Buffalo and Ncome rivers. By now the two men had persuaded themselves that Cetshwayo was only waiting for an opportunity to invade Natal, and that a pre-emptive war would be necessary in order to avoid the worst case scenario of having to fight invading Zulus and rebellious Boers at the same time. So Frere simply suppressed the boundary commission's report long enough for him to find a pretext for the war that would render it irrelevant.

The pretext came in July 1878, when two of the wives of a Zulu chief named Sihayo kaXongo eloped with their lovers into Natal. Sihayo's sons went after them with a band of warriors and brought them back to their father, who executed them. This was not a unique incident, and the execution of the women for adultery, although illegal in Natal, was in accordance with the laws of Zululand. Cetshwayo therefore refused a request for the extradition of the kidnappers. To Sir Bartle Frere this was the excuse he needed. In December he sent Theophilus Shepstone's brother, John, to meet a delegation of Zulu chiefs to discuss the findings of the boundary commission, but this good news for the Zulus was overshadowed by an astonishing ultimatum. Their king was told not only to surrender Sihayo's sons – and pay a fine of cattle for his delay in doing so – but also to disband his army, accept a British resident in his kingdom, and observe the 'promises' supposedly made at his coronation, which among other things involved giving up his power to impose the death penalty on his subjects. The deadline for acceptance of these demands was 11 January 1879. This amounted to a total surrender of Zulu sovereignty and Cetshwayo could not accept it. In fact, of course, he was not intended to; on the British side preparations for war had already begun. As the new year began the regiments of the Zulu Army also began to mobilise.

Looking north-east towards the modern road bridge at Rorke's Drift from a point roughly halfway between the mission station and the river. The 'drift', or ford, in use in 1879 was slightly downstream, to the right. On the far side of the Mzinyathi or Buffalo River is the road to the Batshe Valley and Isandlwana.

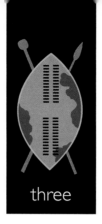

three

The Opposing Armies

In order to understand the campaign that followed it is necessary to know something of the opposing armies. Often seen at the time and later as a clash between 'civilisation' and 'savagery', or 'disciplined' European regulars and 'tribal' warriors, in reality it was nothing of the kind. The great strengths of the British Army had always been its confident sense of superiority, the pride engendered by the traditions of its regimental system, and the self-sacrificing sense of duty of its officer class. In all these respects, the Zulus could match it. Only in technology were they outclassed.

The Zulus

At the root of the disaster at Isandlwana was the British failure to appreciate that the Zulu Army was not like any of the other native African forces that they had previously encountered. Most of the senior British officers as well as many of the rank and file had fought against the Xhosa in the Ninth Cape Frontier War the previous year. The Xhosa were brave and determined fighters, but they remained basically skirmishers uninfluenced by the reforms introduced in Zululand by Shaka. They were grouped into a number of independent clans rather than a coherent nation state, and their chiefs could not exercise the sort of discipline needed to make them charge into the fire of regular infantry at close quarters. They had occasionally tried to emulate European close order tactics, but without success. Battles against the Xhosa had therefore taken the form of long-range exchanges of fire, which the British invariably won. The greatest problems had arisen when the Xhosa avoided battle and resorted to their traditional guerrilla tactics. Not surprisingly, Lord Chelmsford, who had himself led operations against the Xhosa, was heard to comment that his greatest fear now was that the Zulus would not fight.

To those who knew the Zulus better, this was the least of their worries. The Boer veteran J.J. Uys had warned the general that 'the Zulus are more dangerous than you think', but his advice had been ignored. The Zulus did not have a professional standing army like the British, but this did not mean that it was any less well organised or disciplined. Like that of their opponents, the army was based on a regimental system that fostered a strong *esprit de corps*, and commanded by a professional officer corps that could draw on a body of experience and doctrine derived from previous campaigns. A Zulu Army is often referred to by the isiZulu term *impi*, but this is not very precise as it seems to have been used for a body of armed men of any size, from a minor raiding party to the entire fighting force of the kingdom. All Zulu men were enrolled at the age of around 18 into an *ibutho* or regiment (plural *amabutho*), consisting of men of the same age class with whom they would serve for the rest of their lives. When an *ibutho* was formed the king would grant it a title, often suitably warlike, such as the Raisers of Dust or the Humblers of Kings. After a period of military training the new recruits would be allocated their own *kraal*, and would at least in theory be at the disposal of the king until eventually they were granted permission to marry. In practice they might spend two or three months of the year on military duties and be allowed to return home for the rest of the time; this not only made their labour available to their local communities, but spared the king the expense of having to feed them. No man could marry until the king gave his permission to the entire *ibutho*. This often did not happen until the men were in their thirties, although it was not strictly necessary for them to have proved themselves in battle first. Then they would adopt the *isicoco*, or head ring, that denoted their new status, and disperse to establish homes of their own. Married men were, however, still liable to be called up in an emergency, much like the reserves of regular European armies. Putting the married and unmarried regiments together, the total available manpower in 1879 might have comprised as many as 40,000 warriors.

Internally, each regiment was organised into companies, or *amaviyo*, each under a junior officer promoted from among the recruits. The companies were grouped into two 'wings', left and right, commanded – as was the *ibutho* as a whole – by senior officers appointed by the king. Such officers were known as *izinduna* (singular *induna*), though as an *induna* might command a formation of almost any size this title does not correspond precisely to any European rank. Because it was formed of all the men in a certain age group, a Zulu regiment would not be of a standard size and, of course, as its members got older fewer and fewer of them would be fit to take the field. The companies would also vary in strength, generally between about fifty and seventy men. This is one reason why it is difficult to establish the exact size of Zulu armies simply by counting regiments or companies. Traditionally each regiment was distinguished by a unique combination of headgear and other regalia, and by the pattern on its shields. Zulu shields were made from the hides of cattle and retained the animals' natural colouring, of which the local Nguni cattle displayed a great variety. However, by the 1870s most

Zulu warriors depicted by G.F. Angas in *The Kafirs Illustrated* (London, 1849). Although artists often showed them in the elaborate parade costumes that had been introduced under Shaka, by the time of Cetshwayo the Zulus did not wear them into battle. In 1879 they generally fought in nothing more than a loincloth and – for the married men – a head ring.

of the elaborate regalia was worn only on ceremonial occasions, and the warriors went into battle wearing little more than their loincloths, though the married men could still be identified by their head rings. Even the shield patterns may have been less uniform than they had been when the system was established by Shaka, though the general principle still ordained that older veterans carried white shields and younger men black ones – both with variable amounts of patterning in other colours.

In Shaka's day the men had been armed with a large oxhide shield or *isihlangu*, which was almost the height of a man, and a single broad-bladed *iklwa*. The latter weapon is usually referred to in English as an 'assegai', but this is not a Zulu word. All warriors were trained in a close combat drill devised by the king himself, which involved sweeping an opponent's shield aside with the edge of the *isihlangu* and then stabbing him with an underarm thrust to the body. This tactic proved very effective, and to kill his enemy in hand-to-hand combat remained the principal aim of the Zulu warrior. Also useful for this purpose was the *induka* or 'knobkerrie' (another foreign word that has somehow become inseparably associated with the Zulus), a wooden club with a bulbous head that was also carried (and sometimes still is) in civilian life as a walking stick. Throwing spears, which had been banned by Shaka in the belief that stopping to throw missiles would reduce the impetus of the charge, were reintroduced by his successor, Dingaan. Later, in the 1850s, came another change with the introduction of a smaller and handier version of the shield, the *umbhumbuluzo*. Both types were still in use in 1879 but, of course, neither offered much protection against British bullets. During the reigns of Mpande and Cetshwayo the Zulus acquired large numbers of firearms, and it is likely that by 1879 about half the warriors carried a gun as well as the usual spears. However, these were usually obsolete smoothbore muzzle-loaders of a type abandoned in the British Army nearly thirty years before and were far outranged by more modern weapons. Most Zulus were also poor shots, mainly because they lacked enough gunpowder and ammunition to practise. Therefore battlefield tactics remained geared to getting the warriors into hand-to-hand combat, where they could make use of their skill with the stabbing spear.

Senior officers often rode horses, but the Zulu rank and file fought exclusively on foot. Nevertheless, they were lightly equipped and the younger men at least maintained a very high level of physical fitness, so the regiments were highly mobile. In fact, the Boers advised the British to take the same precautions against being outmanoeuvred as if they were facing cavalry. The standard tactical formation – also attributed to Shaka – was known as 'the horns of the bull'. The army would be divided into four sections: a right wing or 'horn', a left 'horn', a centre or 'chest', and a reserve or the 'loins'. The basic plan was that the chest would advance to distract and pin the enemy while the horns spread out and advanced in crescent formations to outflank and encircle him. The loins, meanwhile, would be kept out of the battle unless they were needed to exploit a breakthrough or reinforce one of the other sections. The centre and reserve were usually made up of older more experienced men, while the horns, whose role demanded speed of movement more than steadiness, were formed from the younger unmarried regiments. For an army to rely heavily on a single method of deployment and attack might be thought a source of weakness, but the 'horns of the bull' had stood the Zulus in good stead during Shaka's wars, and would do so again at Isandlwana. It is often argued that at the latter battle it was adopted spontaneously by the individual regiments rather than being planned by the high command, because the fighting developed more or less by accident before the Zulus were ready. However, this proves the value of having such a system of doctrine, which leaves all ranks in no doubt of what they should do even in the absence of specific orders from above. As David Rattray pointed out, it was not only the Zulus' numbers and willingness to fight that defeated Lord Chelmsford: no British general would have imagined that what he regarded as an army of 'savages' could possibly have co-ordinated an encirclement by two wings that had started 5 miles apart. Yet this is exactly what they did at Isandlwana.

In contrast to their tactics, the support services of the Zulu Army were rudimentary and the supply of food was a major weakness. Young boys called *izindibi* were employed to carry rations and sleeping mats for the warriors, but the lack of pack animals or wheeled transport, while contributing to mobility across country, restricted the quantity of supplies that could be carried. So an *impi* could only stay in the field for a short time even if it was victorious in battle. One reason for the attack on Rorke's Drift may have been that the Zulus knew it was a supply base that would contain food. Among the other non-combatants with the army were the doctors or *izinyanga*. Although often disparaged by Europeans with the title of 'witch doctors', they did not rely entirely on magic, but could treat infections with herbs and even perform basic surgery. However, they were not experienced at dealing with the terrible wounds caused when high-velocity bullets struck bone, and there was no organised evacuation procedure after a battle, so that in 1879

The view northwards towards the Batshe Valley from the Rorke's Drift–Isandlwana road. This is the scene that would have greeted the men of Lord Chelmsford's column when they marched into Zululand on 11 January 1879. The openness of the terrain, in contrast to the thick bush in which the previous year's campaign against the Xhosa had been fought, was considered to be an advantage to the British, who failed to appreciate how rapidly the Zulu *impis* could manoeuvre across it.

few of the seriously wounded lived long enough to reach a doctor. The spiritual needs of the troops were ministered to by the *isangoma* or diviner, whose duties included 'doctoring' them before battle by means of special rituals. This was not done before the battles of 22 January because the fight at Isandlwana began prematurely, and some Zulus apparently believed that their high casualty rate was due to the lack of this supernatural protection.

This view, looking south-west from the Isandlwana road on the far side of the river, gives a good idea of the situation of the Rorke's Drift post, which can be seen in the centre of the picture, between Shiyane Hill on the left and the high ground opposite. Behind the post, in the distance, are the heights where the logistic base at Helpmekaar was located.

It does not seem, however, that their morale was adversely affected while the battle was in progress. Fighting on an inauspicious day, without the reassurance of the familiar rituals, with only a rudimentary overall plan against an unfamiliar enemy armed with greatly superior weaponry, the Zulus nevertheless persevered until victory was theirs. Just like the British, they were a fine example of the advantages of self-confidence, discipline and the regimental tradition.

The British

The core of the British forces at Isandlwana and Rorke's Drift consisted of regular infantry from the two battalions of the 24th (2nd Warwickshire) Regiment of Foot. Despite the official county title, infantry regiments at this date did not in practice have a real connection with a particular locality, and recruits might come from all over the country. The 24th's depot had been at Brecon in Wales since 1873, and in 1881, as part of a new policy of giving regiments a local identity, it was retitled the South Wales Borderers. In 1879, however, this was still in the future, and contrary to myth the men of the regiment were not predominantly Welsh. They were, however, mostly veterans of the Ninth Cape Frontier War fought the year before, with useful experience of marching and campaigning in Africa. A regular infantry battalion was composed of eight companies, designated 'A' to 'H', each of which was supposed to consist of about 100 men commanded by a captain. In practice, however, sickness and battle casualties meant that companies were usually seventy to ninety strong, and frequently led by a lieutenant. This was one of the last wars in which the British infantry wore their traditional red coats, and in fact the standard woollen Home Service uniform of red jacket and dark-blue trousers was worn without modification. The only concession to the African climate was a white cork sun helmet, usually stained khaki to make it less conspicuous. The life-sized models in the museum at Rorke's Drift give a good impression of the appearance of the defenders.

The men were armed with the state-of-the-art Martini Henry breech-loading rifle, which had been introduced four years earlier. The weapon had encountered a lot of teething troubles and these are sometimes quoted as

This diorama inside the museum at Rorke's Drift gives a good impression of the difficulty of the attackers' task. Not surprisingly, relatively few of the Zulus ever got close enough to use their stabbing assegais and most of the British casualties were caused by musket balls fired from close range. The appearance of both sides is also depicted fairly accurately. The Zulus have discarded most of their regimental finery and are fighting in simple loincloths, though the married men still wear their head rings. The famous British red coats have begun to fade in the African sun, and the white sun helmets have been dyed brown or khaki to make them less conspicuous.

evidence that the troops in this campaign were let down by their rifles, but in fact the Martini Henry performed extremely well. It was a single-shot weapon, which had to be reloaded by hand every time instead of just by working a bolt like later magazine rifles, but its rate of fire was still a great advance on the clumsy muzzle-loaders on which the Zulus relied. In fact, this rate of fire was seen as a problem at the time, because an excited soldier could easily fire off his personal supply of seventy rounds of ammunition in 10 minutes, at the same time producing enough smoke to blind himself and his officers, because the cartridge still used old-fashioned 'black powder' – smokeless powder being still a decade in the future.

The solution to this problem was to emphasise slow, disciplined firing by volleys at a word of command, but the flat trajectory and sheer power of the Martini Henry bullet meant that even this slow fire was able to stop an attacking enemy at unprecedented distances. Battle accounts from Afghanistan and South Africa often speak of stopping charges in the open at 400 yards, though the particular circumstances at Isandlwana and Rorke's Drift allowed the Zulus to get much closer. Infantry still fought in the traditional two-deep line formation, but this was less rigid than it had been in the Napoleonic era, and a battalion would routinely deploy sections or companies as skirmishers to protect its front, or even form up entirely in what was known as 'extended order' – effectively a long skirmish line with gaps of several yards between each man. This was, of course, more vulnerable than close order if an enemy got to close quarters, but from their experiences in the Cape Frontier War most officers apparently believed that firepower alone would always be able to keep African warriors at a safe distance. If the enemy did close, however, the Martini Henry had one last line of defence in the form of its 22in bayonet, popularly known as a 'lunger', which converted the rifle into a very effective two-handed thrusting weapon. At around 5½ft long this outreached the Zulus' spears in hand-to-hand combat, and could easily penetrate their light oxhide shields. Witnesses from both sides testified to the respect that the Zulus had for the bayonet.

At Isandlwana the defenders of the camp were supported by two 7-pounder rifled muzzle-loading artillery pieces. These were basically light mountain guns on field carriages, each drawn by six horses. They could fire explosive shells, shrapnel or, at close range, case shot, but they were short barrelled and

A portrait of a 'Natal native', from an obviously posed photograph, from the late nineteenth century (Brown). The members of the NNC who fought on the British side in the Anglo-Zulu War would have closely resembled this man, though the extravagant feather headdress is unlikely to have been worn in action.

relatively short ranged, and their influence on the battle was slight. As there was no technique for firing over friendly troops they had to be deployed in the front line, and the Zulus quickly learned to tell when they were about to fire and would take cover before the rounds arrived. One shell exploded short and killed the officer of a friendly cavalry troop, and the guns were eventually overrun as they tried to withdraw to a new position. Even less effective were the 9-pounder Hales rockets that accompanied Colonel Durnford's Number Two Column. These were fired from metal troughs that were much lighter and easier to transport than conventional artillery, and had a respectable range of around 2,000 yards, but they were very inaccurate, sometimes even veering back towards friendly lines. Furthermore, they had no actual warhead, and simply relied on the explosion of unburned propellant to damage the target. Elsewhere in Africa soldiers and explorers valued the psychological effect of rockets on opponents who were unfamiliar with them, but they did not intimidate the Zulus. At Isandlwana the rockets were surprised by enemy skirmishers and the crews shot down before they could get off more than a couple of missiles.

There were no regular cavalry units in this campaign, the mounted arm being supplied by an assortment of mounted infantry, colonial volunteers, police and African levies. (The Lancers and Dragoon Guards who were so successful at the Battle of Ulundi were not deployed to Zululand until after the disaster of Isandlwana.) The Imperial Mounted Infantry was a company-strength unit made up of men from various regular infantry regiments who may have had little experience of horses, but the colonials were competent riders and marksmen, and equipped with breech-loading carbines.

The plain of the Buffalo River, looking west from Shiyane. On the horizon are the hills near the town of Dundee.

Among them were 130 men from the Natal Mounted Police. The largest and most prestigious volunteer unit was the Natal Carbineers, but even this was only about sixty strong. In addition, Colonel Durnford had raised a picked force of African horsemen, also armed with modern breech-loaders, known as the Natal Native Mounted Contingent and consisting of six troops of around fifty men each. Five of these troops were present at Isandlwana. Three were from the amaNgwane tribe led by Chief Zikhali, and were known as Numbers 1 to 3 Troops, Zikhali's Horse; one was the Edendale Troop, made up of Christians from the Edendale Mission, and the fifth consisted of 'Basutos', members of the Sotho people from what is now the state of Lesotho. The latter were so renowned for their horsemanship that it was common for outsiders to refer to all native cavalry as 'Basutos'.

The locally raised infantry, the Natal Native Contingent (NNC), were also recruited by Durnford, but were on the whole less impressive. They were drawn mainly from groups that had originally arrived in Natal as refugees from the Zulus. They had no recent military experience and were very sketchily trained in British drill and tactics. Altogether there were seven battalions, each of ten companies, but these varied widely in actual strength. As the white settlers were worried about encouraging an insurrection, only one man in ten was allowed a rifle, the rest having to rely on their traditional spears and shields. Many of their white officers and NCOs were themselves inexperienced, and few of them spoke any African language or had any understanding of their culture. Not surprisingly the NNC were very reluctant to face the Zulus in battle. One exception was the three companies of the isiGqoza contingent, drawn from the Zulu clan that had been defeated in the civil war of 1856, who were well motivated and accustomed to fighting in Zulu style.

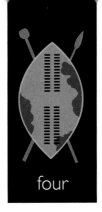

four

The Campaign Begins

Few of the British officers and men who marched into Zululand at the beginning of 1879 can have expected to encounter serious opposition on the battlefield. After their experiences with Xhosa ambushes in the Cape Frontier War they no doubt looked at the grassy plains of Zululand with a sense of relief; there would be few opportunities for the Zulus to skirmish from cover, and if they tried to close in in the open they would surely be beaten by superior firepower. Right on schedule, on 11 January, the first British forces began to move into Zululand. Their commander-in-chief was Lieutenant General Frederick Thesiger, 2nd Baron Chelmsford, a career soldier in his early fifties who had distinguished himself in the Abyssinian campaign of 1868, and more recently in the war against the Xhosa in the Eastern Cape, which had ended in 1878. Chelmsford divided his forces into five columns, of which three marched into Zululand while the other two guarded the Natal border against invasion. The objective of all three attacking forces was Cetshwayo's capital at Ulundi, about 100km from the frontier. Number One column, under Colonel Charles Pearson, crossed into Zululand via the Lower Drift on the Thukela River, at the eastern end of the front near the coast. On the north-western flank was Colonel Evelyn Wood's Number Four column, while in the centre Colonel Richard Glyn of the 24th Foot led the Centre, or Number Three, column across the Buffalo River at Rorke's Drift and Colonel Anthony Durnford's Number Two column remained in reserve. Number Three column consisted of approximately 4,700 men, comprising the two regular infantry battalions of the 24th Regiment of Foot; around 2,000 auxiliaries of the 3rd Regiment, NNC, in two battalions; six 7-pounder guns; and five units of mounted Natal Volunteers drawn from the white settler population. The supply train consisted of more than 300 wagons, drawn by 1,500 oxen and more than 100 pack mules and horses.

The Buffalo River, looking upstream from the Rorke's Drift Bridge. This pool is where Lieutenant Chard's ponts were situated. This photograph was taken in late October. In January, just as at Fugitives' Drift, the water would usually be higher and the current faster.

Looking south-east from the same viewpoint as the previous photograph. The lower slopes of Shiyane Hill – known to the British at the time of the battle as the Oskarberg – can be seen on the right. In the middle distance at centre right is Rorke's Drift Hotel. The line of greenery marks the course of the Buffalo River. Behind the bend of the river, in the distance, is the distinctive silhouette of Isandlwana. Note, however, that Isandlwana is not visible from the mission station itself because of the intervening peak of Shiyane.

The pool and the ford at Rorke's Drift, from the slopes of Shiyane. The original crossing point was just downstream of the bridge (towards the camera), where the river runs through the rocky shallows. Chard's ponts were moored in the pool on the far side of the modern bridge.

Rorke's Drift was a site of immense strategic importance. Not only was it one of only a handful of places where an army of this size could cross the Buffalo and Thukela rivers, which formed the boundary of the Zulu kingdom, but it was a vital link in the supply chain between the front line and the main logistic base at Helpmekaar, which was about 8km away to the south-west at the top of a steep hill. The tiny settlement at the Drift was located at the base of Shiyane Hill, on the Natal side of the Buffalo. It consisted of a dwelling house and a storehouse, and had been built in the 1850s by Jim Rorke, who owned a farm in the area but made his living mainly by hunting and trading with the Zulus across the river. Rorke had died in 1875 and the place had eventually been bought by a Swedish missionary, Otto Witt, from whom the British Army had requisitioned it. In January 1879 it was packed with

Looking north-eastwards up the Batshe Valley to the scene of the engagement of 12 January that ended with the burning of Chief Sihayo's *kraal* by the British. On the right is the escarpment along which Lord Chelmsford's mounted troops made their outflanking move, and up which the Zulus eventually retired. The *kraal* itself is hidden behind a spur running down from the escarpment in the distance.

supplies of mealie meal and biscuit. 'Mealie' was the local term for maize flour, which was packed in sacks weighing 200lb each, the famous 'mealie bags' that were to make such a vital contribution to the defence of Rorke's Drift. The supplies were guarded by a garrison consisting of two companies – B Company, 2nd Battalion, 24th Foot, commanded by Lieutenant Gonville Bromhead, and a several-hundred-strong company of 2nd/3rd NNC under Captain William Stephenson. There were also around thirty sick men in the Reverend Witt's house, which had been converted into a hospital. January is the rainy season in Zululand and the river was high, so despite the existence of the ford (or 'drift' to use the local term) it was necessary to ferry the regular infantry over on 'ponts', or ferries hauled across by ropes. (The NNC auxiliaries had to either wade or swim, and several of them were drowned.) The crossing was unopposed, but it took all day and part of the next to get the transport across. The garrison at Rorke's Drift was supplemented by half a dozen Royal Engineers under Lieutenant John Chard, whose job it was to maintain the ponts. The officer in overall command of the post was Major Henry Spalding, Number Three column's Deputy Assistant Adjutant-General, who was responsible for the supply lines between Helpmekaar and the fighting units.

The Battle of the Batshe Valley

Lord Chelmsford's plan was to turn east after crossing the river and march immediately on Ulundi. However, no more than 5km from the Drift the trail led across the Batshe River, just downstream of the *kraal* of Chief Sihayo kaXongo. Not only was Sihayo, in the British view, partly to blame for the war, but he presented a potential threat to the left flank of the column. On 12 January the commander-in-chief therefore led a detachment to attack the *kraal*. This consisted mainly of units of the NNC, perhaps chosen for the job partly so that the senior officers could observe their performance. Today a panoramic view of the Batshe Valley battlefield can be obtained from the Rorke's Drift–Isandlwana road. The Zulus, led by Sihayo's son, Mkhumbikazulu, took up a defensive position in thick scrub at the base of a semicircular recess in the cliffs leading up to the ridge. It was here that the famous exchange took place recorded by Commandant George Hamilton Browne, commanding the 1st/3rd NNC. A Zulu warrior called out to the advancing British, asking by whose orders they had come to Zululand: an officer who spoke the language replied, 'By the orders of the Great White Queen!' Browne's battalion then advanced, but was met by heavy fire that drove most of the NNC to ground. Their commander and three isiGqoza companies continued to skirmish forward while Major Black of the 2nd/24th rallied the waverers, and the mounted units outflanked the enemy via the top

A closer view of the recess in the cliffs on the eastern side of the Batshe Valley, where the fight took place between Sihayo's men and the NNC. The main features of this battlefield can be easily seen from the Isandlwana road.

of the ridge. Eventually the Zulu position at the foot of the cliff was taken, though most of the defenders escaped over the top. Thanks to poor Zulu marksmanship the column's casualties were only a few men wounded, while around thirty Zulus were killed, including Mkhumbikazulu. The British went on to burn Sihayo's *kraal*, steal his livestock and declare a victory. This first clash might have alerted them to the fact that the enemy would put up a more determined resistance than expected, but if anything it confirmed their already overconfident assessment of the Zulus.

The Advance to Isandlwana

From the Batshe Valley a track ran eastwards in the direction of Ulundi, but within the first few miles it crossed two sizeable streams whose boggy banks were unsuitable for wagons. It took a week for Chelmsford's engineers to improve the road to the required standard, which explains why it was not until 20 January that Number Three Column's main camp could be moved forward from Rorke's Drift. The site chosen for the next camp was at the base of the distinctively shaped hill known as Isandlwana, about ten miles to the east, which is easily visible from vantage points along the road. Isandlwana is a steep sided rocky 'kopje' or 'koppie', of a type not uncommon in South Africa, and is not especially high. It is overlooked by the Nqutu Plateau a mile to the north, and is slightly smaller than the hill known as Shiyane above Rorke's Drift. But something about its shape and relative isolation made Isandlwana a landmark long before it acquired its modern, slightly sinister associations. To the more imaginative of the men of the 24th it seemed to resemble the Sphinx insignia on the regiment's cap badge. Various translations of the Zulu name have appeared in print over the years, and the question is discussed in detail by Ian Knight in his *Companion to the Anglo-Zulu War* (Pen & Sword, 2008). All we really need to know is sources that render it as 'a little hut' or 'the second stomach of a cow' are probably both correct, since in isiZulu the same term can be used for both.

Much has been written about the unsuitability of the site for a camp, but without the benefit of hindsight it must have seemed an excellent choice. It had good lines of sight in most directions – especially to the east, the direction in which the enemy army was thought to be – and was close to a source of water and firewood in the Manzimnyama River. It was not, in any case, intended to be occupied for more than a few days. For this reason no attempt was made to fortify it. Friendly Boers such as J.J. Uys had advised the British to protect all their camps with a ring of laagered wagons, but the wagon train was still needed to bring up supplies, and the risk of an attack was obviously considered to be negligible. Later versions of the official

A classic view of Isandlwana Hill from the west. Troops approaching from this direction were struck by the resemblance to the Egyptian Sphinx, which featured on the cap badge of the 24th Foot.

Regulations for Field Forces in South Africa did instruct field commanders to *laager*, but the lesson was learned too late for many of the men who pitched their tents here on the evening of 20 January. Although the view to the east is extensive, there are many undulations in the ground that are hard to see from Isandlwana, leaving the viewer with the general impression that he can see a lot more than he actually can. At the eastern end of the valley is a series of hills known as the Mangeni Range that could easily conceal hostile forces; in fact, unknown to the British, the main Zulu Army was hidden somewhere on the far left of the hills, behind a spur known as Itusi that projected into the plain from the escarpment of the Nqutu Plateau to the north. Lord Chelmsford therefore ordered a reconnaissance in force early in the morning of 21 January, sending out most of the mounted troops,

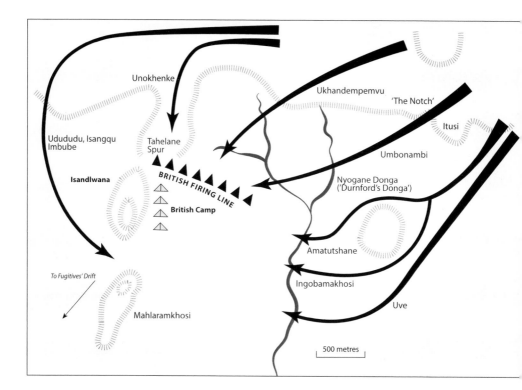

Sketch map of the Battle of Isandlwana.

supported by the 1st and 2nd Battalions of the 3rd NNC, under Major J.G. Dartnell to patrol the hills. It is interesting to note that Chelmsford was also worried about the security of his southern flank, along the valley of the Buffalo River, because he had despatched Major Harcourt Bengough with the 2nd/1st NNC to advance along this axis. The one place that was not reconnoitred properly was beyond the opposite flank, on the plateau.

At first there was no sign of the enemy, but towards the end of the day Major Dartnell encountered a force of several hundred Zulus on the Hlazakazi Heights. At first they looked as if they were going to attack, but then fell back and disappeared behind a hill. Dartnell's orders were to return to camp after his reconnaissance, but he was reluctant to lose contact with what he probably thought was the main enemy army, especially as it seemed to be retreating. So he stayed where he was when night fell, within sight of the Zulu camp fires, and sent a messenger to the general asking for reinforcements. When Chelmsford got the message, around 2 a.m. on 22 January, his main concern was that the enemy might escape. He therefore gathered a scratch force consisting of most of the 2nd/24th, the mounted troops, and four of the six artillery pieces in the camp, and marched out before dawn. Because of the need for haste all the baggage and equipment, including the reserve ammunition, was left in the camp. As an afterthought he sent an order to Colonel Durnford's Number Two Column, which was then at Rorke's Drift, to advance to Isandlwana. Not long after dawn Chelmsford caught up with Dartnell on the Hlazakazi Heights, only to find that the enemy opposite him had disappeared. Opinions differ as to whether the Zulus had deliberately decoyed the general into thinking that their main force was in the east while they outflanked him to the north. There is no firm evidence that it was deliberate, but we need to bear in mind that the Zulu Army did not issue written orders, and that most of their senior commanders were killed during the war or shortly afterwards without having left an account of their actions. Hard evidence for exactly what their plans and intentions were is therefore never going to be easy to find. But whether it was the result of a deliberate ploy or not, the effect was the same. The British had divided their forces in proximity to a more mobile enemy, without having established where that enemy's main army was.

ORDERS OF BATTLE, ISANDLWANA, 22 JANUARY 1879

The Zulus

Ntshingwayo kaMahole
Mavumengwana kaNdlela

Right Horn:
uDududu Regiment
iMbube Regiment
iSangqu Regiment

Chest:
uNokhenke Regiment
uKhandempemvu Regiment
uMbonambi Regiment

Left Horn:
uVe Regiment
iNgobamakhosi Regiment

Loins:
uThulwana Regiment (M)
uDloko Regiment (M)
iNdlondlo Regiment (M)
iNdluyengwe Regiment

(M) denotes a married (or senior) regiment.

The uKhandempemvu Regiment is often referred to by its alternative (but to an English speaker virtually unpronounceable) title of umCijo.

Detachments from other regiments may also have been present, bringing the total of combatants up to about 24,000, of whom 19,000 were actually engaged.

The British

Lieutenant Colonel H.B. Pulleine (Detachment from No. 3 Column)

1st Battalion, 24th Foot (Captain W. Degacher):
A Company (Lieutenant C.W. Cavaye)
C Company (Captain R. Younghusband)
E Company (Lieutenant F.P. Porteous)
F Company (Captain W.E. Mostyn)
H Company (Captain G.V. Wardell)

G Company, 2nd Battalion, 24th Foot (Lieutenant C. Pope)

1st Battalion, 3rd Natal Native Contingent:
No. 6 Company (Captain Krohn)
No. 9 Company (Captain Lonsdale)

2nd Battalion, 3rd NNC:
No. 4 Company (Captain Erskine)
No. 5 Company (Captain Barry)

Mounted detachments from:
No. 1 Squadron, Mounted Infantry
Natal Carbineers
Natal Mounted Police
Newcastle Mounted Rifles
Buffalo Border Guard

Two 7-pounder guns of N Battery, 5 Brigade, Royal Artillery (Major S. Smith)

Plus various attached staff officers, medical orderlies, transport drivers, pioneers, etc.

Colonel A.W. Durnford (Detachment from No. 2 Column)

(Colonel Durnford was senior to Pulleine, but had no responsibility for the camp. See the text for the attempts to blame Durnford for the defeat, and the controversy that this still causes.)

Mounted Troops (Captain W. Barton)
Edendale Troop, Basuto Troop (Lieutenant A.F. Henderson)
No. 1 Troop, Zikhali's Horse (Lieutenant C. Raw)
No. 2 Troop, Zikhali's Horse (Lieutenant J.A. Roberts)
No. 3 Troop, Zikhali's Horse (Lieutenant R.W. Vause)

1st Battalion, 1st Natal Native Contingent:
D Company (Captain Nourse)
E Company (Captain Stafford)

Three 9-pounder rocket launchers of 11 Battery, 7 Brigade Royal Artillery (Major F.B. Russell)

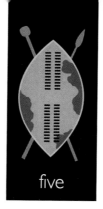

five

The Battle of Isandlwana

Back at the camp beneath Isandlwana, another problem was becoming apparent to at least some of the British officers. Without the companies that the commander-in-chief had taken away, there were not enough men to defend its perimeter in the event of a serious attack. Colonel Pulleine, left in command, already knew that there was a risk of an attack because several parties of Zulus had been seen during the early part of the morning moving about on the Nqutu Plateau. Durnford's column arrived about 11 a.m., but its commander interpreted his rather vague orders as requiring him to press on and join up with Chelmsford. In fact, far from reinforcing the camp, he asked for two more companies of the 24th to go with him – a request that Pulleine prudently refused. Replying that he would expect support if he got into trouble, Durnford rode off down the valley, detaching two troops of Zikhali's Horse under lieutenants Roberts and Raw to scout the Nqutu Plateau on his left. Some have argued that Durnford was mostly to blame for the subsequent disaster, by not only advancing his own troops into an untenable position but obliging Pulleine to spread his own men out to support him. Certainly by the time the Zulus attacked both British columns had become spread out in a very haphazard fashion over several miles of countryside. But it was Chelmsford who had started that particular trend, and by not giving Durnford precise orders he had compounded his original mistake. We might speculate on what would have happened if the Zulus had been planning to attack Chelmsford's left flank instead of the camp, and Durnford had arrived just in time to forestall them. There was an unseemly row after the battle when Chelmsford's Chief of Staff, Lieutenant Colonel Crealock, claimed to have issued Durnford with orders to take command of the camp, only

Looking south-east from the mission station there is a good view of the country to the east of the camp at Isandlwana. Note the conical hill known as Amatutshane, at centre left. In the distance are the Mangeni Hills, where Major Dartnell made contact with what he thought was the main Zulu Army on the evening of 21 January. The modern church is visible in the right foreground.

for the orders in question to be found on Durnford's body and shown to have contained no such instruction. Pro- and anti-Durnford parties have continued to argue ever since, with one side contending that he was made a scapegoat, and the other that he was known to be rash and insubordinate. It is fair enough to say, however, that his arrival at Isandlwana triggered a series of events that he could hardly have been expected to foresee.

Firstly, it seems to have encouraged Pulleine to disperse his forces, sending companies further out to the north and east than he need have done just to defend the camp. Then, with the 24th having lost the opportunity to make a concentrated stand in square at the camp – which, had they known it, was the defenders' only chance – Durnford's scouts set off the avalanche. Two days earlier the Zulu Army had been where Chelmsford thought it was, to the east around Siphezi Mountain, but while Dartnell was skirmishing with what turned out to be its flank guards, the main force had broken contact and marched north-westwards to a position on the Nqutu Plateau on the left flank of the British line of advance. Standing on the plain near Isandlwana and looking eastwards, it is hard to believe that this manoeuvre could have been carried out without being noticed, as there appears to be an uninterrupted line of sight all the way to Siphezi and beyond. But in fact there is plenty of dead ground in which troops could be concealed, and the British patrols had failed to spot the Zulu movements in this vital sector. Much of the credit for this must surely go to the man in command of the Zulu scouts, Zibhebhu kaMapitha, who took up arms against his king during the civil wars of the early 1880s, but was to gain a reputation as the best Zulu general of the period.

It was later confirmed by Zulu witnesses that Ntshingwayo kaMahole, who was in command of the Zulu Army, did not intend to give battle on 22 January, if only because it was an inauspicious day to his people – the 'day of the dead moon'. (This is what is known in English as a 'new moon', when the moon is at the stage in its cycle when it is not visible.) Neither is the Zulu general likely to have foreseen that Lord Chelmsford would divide his column, or that Durnford's orders would lead to a further scattering of the remaining defenders of the camp. But by placing himself undetected on the flank of any future British advance he had already gained an important strategic advantage. Perhaps he intended to assault the camp at dawn on the following day, or to descend on Number Three Column while it was on the march and immobilise it by capturing its transport. Another of the controversies surrounding this battle concerns exactly where the Zulus were encamped on the morning of 22 January. The most popular choice is the Ngwebeni Valley, about 6km north-east of Isandlwana, though Mike Snook has pointed out that there was no room in the valley for an *impi* of 25,000 men to deploy into battle formation. So the right horn was probably

From slightly higher up the slope on which the mission station is situated a clearer view of the western part of the plain can be obtained. Beyond the prominent ridge in the centre left the ground falls away into the Mangeni Gorge, the site of the spectacular Mangeni Falls. It was in this area that Lord Chelmsford was searching for the Zulu Army when the camp was attacked.

already somewhere to the west, and already moving further out to take up a position from which it could swing behind Isandlwana and cut off any British retreat. In fact, there must have been troop movements in several localities on the plateau during the morning, some of which had been spotted from below by the British. It might have been in response to one such sighting, or perhaps rather later in an effort to protect Durnford's flank, that Pulleine sent Lieutenant Cavaye's A Company of the 1st/24th up on to the plateau.

Amatutshane, seen from the Isandlwana mission. During the battle the Zulu right horn swept from left to right round the far side of Amatutshane to threaten the exposed flank of Colonel Durnford's mounted troops, while their centre advanced from left to right across the intervening low ground towards the British camp.

They occupied a spur of high ground called Tahelane that runs down towards Isandlwana Hill. Already on the plateau was a company of the NNC under Captain Barry, occupying a high point called Mkwene about half a mile further out.

Not long after 11 a.m., just after Durnford had moved out from the camp, the troopers under Raw and Roberts, while chasing a group of Zulus who were driving off cattle, unexpectedly blundered into the Zulu chest sheltering in the Ngwebeni Valley. Different sources describe the warriors as either sitting on the ground or already on the move in long lines, a discrepancy that can be explained by the presence of several distinct bodies of men in the area, but the uKhandempemvu regiment, which was closest to the astonished cavalrymen, does seem to have been taken by surprise. At once the warriors stood up and charged, while their comrades in the uMbonambi and uNokhenke, anxious not to miss the action, deployed into line on their left and right respectively. Precisely where the iNgobamakhosi and uVe regiments had been bivouacked is not clear, but they now moved out to the east to form the left horn, with the younger and quicker warriors of the uVe at the tip. It is unlikely that Ntshingwayo or any other senior *induna* was able to direct or control all these movements, but the deployment was in accordance with standard Zulu doctrine and the regimental officers probably did not need specific orders. Somewhere to the rear were the four veteran regiments constituting the Zulu loins, but most of these men were restrained by their officers from joining the headlong advance, though a few, eager for glory, managed to join the units of the left horn. Meanwhile Raw and Roberts' men were falling back in front of the Zulus, dismounting every so often to fire volleys from their carbines, but without any realistic hope of stopping them. Eventually they ran into Barry's NNC, who fled in panic. No doubt hearing the commotion, the Zulu right horn also moved out from their hiding places to spring their part of the trap.

Up on Tahelane, Cavaye's men saw part of the right horn moving from right to left across their front at a range of about 800 yards and opened fire on it, though to little effect as the range was too great. Colonel Pulleine heard the firing and sent another company, F, under Captain Mostyn, to reinforce Cavaye. By now the position on the spur north of the camp was being held by two companies of British infantry, three troops of Zikhali's

Horse (those of Raw and Roberts plus a third that had come up from the camp to assist them) and some of Barry's NNC, who had managed to rally behind the friendly troops. The defenders also had the support of Pulleine's two artillery pieces, which were deployed facing north on the plain about 500 yards east of the camp. However, although the guns were well placed to fire on any enemy coming down the escarpment from the plateau, they could not see the Zulus threatening Mostyn and Cavaye. Their right flank was also

The escarpment marking the edge of the Nqutu Plateau, looking north from the area of the British camp beneath Isandlwana. This photograph was taken in October. At this time of year the grass is dry and sparse, and the features of the battlefield are easier to see; in January, when the battle was fought, the grass was taller and provided better cover for the Zulu advance.

dangerously exposed. To the officers and men in the camp the situation at this point cannot have seemed very serious, but in fact the defenders were already doomed. There were simply not enough men to check the Zulu centre and both horns, which were now moving into position to outflank and eventually surround them. Their only chance might have been if Lord Chelmsford had brought his part of the column back at once to help them, but the commander-in-chief had no idea that there was a problem. In fact,

The spur of the plateau on which A and F Companies of the 1st/24th were deployed when the Zulu attack began, looking south-westwards towards Rorke's Drift. Lieutenant Cavaye's A Company, deployed on the edge of the flat ground to the right, opened fire at 800 yards range on the Zulu right horn as it passed across their front. The British defenders later retreated towards the bottom left of the picture in the direction of the camp. Isandlwana is just out of shot on the left.

he had just sent a messenger to Pulleine with orders to strike the camp and advance to join him – orders that the colonel was forced to ignore as more and more of his units were sucked into the fighting on the plateau.

Meanwhile, Durnford's cavalry had gone east for about 4 miles until they were out of sight of the camp, leaving the rocket battery and its NNC escort far behind in their headlong advance. Durnford was warned by messengers from Raw and Roberts of the Zulu presence on his left flank, but it was

The road up the escarpment onto the Nqutu Plateau, seen from the vicinity of the Isandlwana battlefield site.

not until the main body of the uVe appeared a few hundred yards in front, moving across his line of march, that he realised he would have to retreat. Using the usual tactic of dismounting to fire and then falling back, he reached the dry watercourse known locally as Nyogane – often referred to today as Durnford's '*donga*' – which ran roughly north to south across the plain below the slopes of a conical hill called Amatutshane, about half a mile from the camp. Here he prepared to make a stand. The men of the rocket battery, still isolated on the open plain behind him, stood no chance. When the iNgobamakhosi came into view over the lip of the plateau they were little more than 100 yards away, and although the artillerymen got off at least one rocket and briefly forced the enemy to take cover, they were quickly shot down by close range musket fire. Their commander, Major Russell, was killed, the NNC escort fled, and the survivors, rallied by Captain Nourse, fell back towards the camp with Durnford's retreating troopers covering their escape. In fact, the rockets – deployed partly with the idea of intimidating an 'unsophisticated' African enemy – do not seem to have impressed the Zulus at all. According to A. W. Lee (quoted in Ian Knight's *Companion to the Anglo-Zulu War*) someone in the ranks of the iNgobamakhosi even improvised a poem on the spot, playing on the resemblance between the isiZulu word for 'heaven' and the name of the *amaZulu* themselves: 'Lightning, lightning of heaven, it glitters and shines; Sun, sun of the Zulus, it consumes all.'

It was now about noon, and Colonel Pulleine must by this time have realised the extent of the threat from the north, because he rearranged the camp's defenders into a new firing line facing the escarpment, with E and H Companies, 1st/24th, on either side of the two guns, and G Company 2nd/24th, under Lieutenant Pope, further out to the right. The units on the Tahelane Spur were then brought down to extend the left, with C Company 1st/24th on the far left, echeloned slightly back. Several writers have pointed out that this deployment conformed closely to the defensive formation prescribed in Lord Chelmsford's instructions issued before the campaign. There was, however, one crucial difference: the original orders described a second line of regular infantry forming a reserve, but this line did not exist at Isandlwana. About 500 yards beyond the camp a low ridge running across the plain created a dangerous area of dead ground beyond it, so the British line appears to have been advanced on to the forward slope of this ridge, where recent archaeological surveys have found large numbers of Martini Henry cartridges. The three regiments of the Zulu chest responded to the British withdrawal from the plateau by attempting to charge over the crest and down towards the camp, but the British had carried out the manoeuvre in good order and responded with volleys of rifle fire. These inflicted heavy casualties, and forced the Zulus to go to ground about 300 yards short of the British line. Visitors to the battlefield should remember that although for

Slightly to the right of Amatutshane when seen from Isandlwana, the *donga* in which Colonel Durnford attempted to make a stand runs across the picture from near the buildings at bottom left, approximately 700m east of the camp.

Isandlwana from the north, seen from the Nqutu Plateau road. This is the view that the warriors of the Zulu chest must have had as they descended the escarpment. Their task was made slightly easier by the cover provided by the long grass and the low rocky ridge – not very prominent from this angle – which runs from left to centre right in the middle distance. The scattered white dots to the left of the hill are the cairns that mark the burial sites of the British troops. They indicate roughly the area of the British camp and the last stand. The modern mission station and museum are marked by the purple jacaranda trees at bottom right. The overall impression from here is that the camp was not poorly sited, as is often alleged. The only direction in which a possible attack would have been hidden by the hill itself is along the road from Rorke's Drift – an unlikely line of approach and one that could have been covered by lookouts on top of the hill. As the Zulus had no artillery they could not threaten the camp directly from this position on the ridge. Lines of sight in other directions, especially to the east, are as good as can be found anywhere in the area.

most of the year the grass is sparse and provides little cover, in a wet January it can grow thickly to a height of several feet, so an opponent lying down in it would be virtually invisible even at relatively close range.

Meanwhile, Durnford's troopers were also keeping their opponents of the uVe regiment at a distance with their carbines until their ammunition began to run short. The traditional story that the battle was lost because the British ran out of ammunition, or the quartermasters refused to release it, has long since been disproved, but the men of Zikhali's Horse detailed to bring extra rounds up to the firing line in the *donga* did undoubtedly have a frustrating time. They were a long way from their wagons, and did not know where they had been left in the chaos of the morning's hasty advance, while the quartermasters of the 24th were naturally reluctant to issue their own unit's ammunition to men they did not know. Durnford's position had in any case been turned by this time as the Zulu left horn swept round his open right flank, and about 1.15 p.m. he gave the order to resume the retirement towards the camp. Unfortunately, Pope's company – either spontaneously or under orders from Pulleine – had just begun to move further to the right to support Durnford, whose sudden withdrawal left Pope dangerously exposed. At about the same time Ntshingwayo realised that the attack of the Zulu chest had stalled, and sent an *induna* named Mkhosana kaMvundlana forward to rally them. This officer – one of the true unsung heroes of the battle – strode upright along the line despite the British fire, reminding the uKhandempemvu of their king's orders and of the boasts that the warriors had made before the battle. Kipling famously described the Beja 'Fuzzy Wuzzies' of the Sudan as 'the only thing that doesn't give a damn' for a regiment of British infantry. But the men of the uKhandempemvu and uMbonambi regiments were certainly not overawed either. They rose to their feet and charged, closely followed by their comrades on either side. Mkhosana charged with them, only to be shot dead before he could reach the enemy. But in a matter of minutes what had seemed a secure British position was on the verge of collapse. The 7-pounder guns in the centre fired a couple of rounds of canister, but to little effect; the Zulus had observed that the crews stepped away from the guns when they were about to fire, and this gave them enough warning to dive for cover. Between the shots the Zulus came on so fast that Major Smith only just managed to limber the guns and gallop off before they were captured; one gunner was actually stabbed to death before he could mount his horse.

We should not imagine that the 1st/24th was overwhelmed in the next few minutes, although some early accounts – written, inevitably, by those who had left the field well before the end – do give that impression. Neither is the explanation for the defeat given in the report of the court of inquiry

Looking from the *nek* towards the cairns marking H Company's stand and the position of the original British firing line beyond, with the lip of the Nqutu Plateau on the horizon. The cairns dotting this area probably mark the spots where soldiers were overtaken and killed during the retirement to the camp.

Isandlwana Hill, from a nineteenth-century photograph. (Brown)

Looking from the camp towards the 'notch' in the escarpment, with Amatutshane Hill just out of shot to the right. The British firing line was along the ridge discernible in the middle distance. The regiments of the Zulu chest descended the escarpment here in open order, under fire from Major Smith's two guns, but went to ground at the bottom under heavy British rifle fire before rallying for the final charge.

held after the battle likely to be true. This report, and the subsequent official 'Narrative of Field Operations', claimed that the British line had been holding well until a body of NNC troops in the centre fled in panic. It is true that most of the NNC were neither well-armed nor highly motivated, but that is one reason why no competent commander would have relied on them to hold the centre of the line in the first place. In fact, we can be fairly confident that at this stage of the battle most of the NNC who had not already run away were deployed on the right flank or in the camp to the rear.

Looking north across the *nek* towards Isandlwana Hill from near the car park, with the memorial to the 24th Foot at centre right.

Neither is it true that the regulars ran out of ammunition, nor that the lids of the boxes that held the reserve rounds for the Martini Henrys were screwed down, making their contents inaccessible. Even if the battalion's pioneer section had not had such a thing as a screwdriver, in an emergency like this the boxes would surely have yielded to the butt or bayonet of a rifle. The truth is that the British firing line was doomed even before the final Zulu charge, because its flanks were already being enveloped and there were no reserves available to secure them. Their only chance would have been to

From the site of the cairns, looking in the direction from which the Zulu chest and left horn made their final advance.

The largest concentration of cairns is on the eastern slope of the *nek*, seen here from the base of the hill.

This collection of cairns about 200m south-east of the hill probably marks the location of one of the 'solid squares' of British infantry that Zulu eyewitnesses recalled making a final stand on the *nek*. This square may have consisted largely of the survivors of H Company, with elements of other units picked up as they retreated through the camp. There are also colonial troops buried at this spot, which is therefore often identified as a possible site for Durnford's last stand. The Zulus were kept at bay for a while by the bayonets of the regulars, but they eventually overwhelmed them with a hail of thrown spears. Note the monument to the 24th on the horizon at centre left. Halfway up the hill in the centre can be seen the cairn marking the position of C Company's last stand.

form a close order square in the camp and fortify it with the wagons, in Boer style, but it was now too late even for that desperate measure.

What now seems to have happened is that the various units on the British side fell back independently towards the camp while the Zulus streamed through the gaps between them, the men of both sides becoming increasingly mixed up as they reached the tents. Normally these would have been struck in order to provide a clear field of fire for the defenders, but this had not

Numerous whitewashed cairns dot the battlefield, each marking a mass grave where the British and colonial dead were buried. However, the site has been reorganised and some of the dead reburied on several occasions, and the memorials erected later to the various units involved do not necessarily indicate the exact locations where they made their last stands.

been done, and the defence was now in utter chaos. The artillery galloped into the camp and simply kept going, though those gunners who had not been able to mount were quickly killed. Most of the remaining NNC also made their escape. Durnford, to his credit, did not; he stayed to support the Carbineers on the right of the line, and was killed there with most of his troopers. Of the regular infantry companies, Pope's G Company was the most exposed and was apparently overwhelmed out on the plain before it

The memorial to the 24th Foot on the field of Isandlwana was erected to commemorate the dead of both Isandlwana and Rorke's Drift. Near this spot E and F Companies 1st/24th made their final stand after their retreat from the firing line.

could get back to the camp. Those who had been holding the centre of the line facing the plateau retired in something like good order to a position just beneath Isandlwana Hill, but here they were split up into small groups, surrounded by the warriors of the Zulu chest and forced to make a stand. In places on the battlefield it is still possible to identify the spots where they stood and died. According to Zulu participants they continued to fight courageously, but with access to the ammunition in the camp cut off they

Looking down from Isandlwana Hill across the *nek*, where the retreating British found their escape blocked by the Zulu right horn, towards the 24th Regiment's memorial. Mahlbamkhosi Hill, known to the British as the 'stony koppie', rises behind the car park. Below the hill to the left, near the red buildings, the memorial to the Natal Carbineers marks the area where, according to one interpretation of the evidence, Colonel Durnford made his last stand with the colonial troops against the uVe and iNgobamakhosi Regiments of the Zulu left horn.

did eventually run out of rounds for the Martini Henrys, and were forced to rely on bayonets and the officers' revolvers. Even then they were not easily destroyed, because the rifle and bayonet had a longer reach than the Zulu assegais and many of the enemy who tried to close with them were killed, but their determination could only postpone the end. Finally the Zulus broke up their formations with a shower of thrown spears, then charged into the gaps to finish off the survivors.

The upper slopes of Isandlwana Hill seen from the south-east. According to Zulu eyewitnesses Captain Younghusband's C Company charged down in this direction to their deaths from the shoulder in the foreground.

Meanwhile, Younghusband's C Company, which had been holding the far left of the line, had managed to get on to the hill itself and take cover behind the boulders that littered its slopes. From here they held off the enemy for some time, until they too ran out of ammunition. The Zulus said that they paused in their attacks while the young officer shook hands with his men. Younghusband then led them in a final charge, swinging his sword around his head as described graphically by a Zulu eyewitness, but they had no chance of breaking through and were all killed on the plain below. The isiGqoza, disdaining to run from their traditional enemies while they had ammunition left, also made a last stand on the hill, and died just as heroically. Even then a collection of survivors from the shattered British units was trying to rally on the *nek* or saddle south of Isandlwana, but they found themselves directly in the path of the Zulu right horn as it swept round the hill from the west. According to another Zulu account, the very last British survivor was an unidentified infantryman who holed up in a cave on Isandlwana and kept his attackers at bay for 2 hours with his rifle, until at last the Zulus collected a number of captured Martini Henrys and concentrated their fire into the cave until there was no sign of life. Much has been made of the fact that a partial eclipse of the sun occurred around the time of the last stand, but it

The last stand of the 24th at Isandlwana as imagined by a nineteenth-century artist. (Brown)

The memorial to the Natal Mounted Police, erected in 1913.

is unlikely that the brief dimming of the sunlight was noticeable amid the smoke of battle, though observers further away did record it. (Incidentally the eclipse has nothing to do with the 'dead moon' that made the day an inauspicious one from the Zulu point of view. It is true that a solar eclipse can only happen at the time of a new moon, but the latter is a regular and easily predictable event, whereas an eclipse is not.) Altogether casualties on the British side at Isandlwana amounted to around 710 regulars, 150 white South Africans and more than 400 African auxiliaries – the worst disaster to befall Queen Victoria's armies since the retreat from Kabul in 1842. The Zulu casualties were not recorded, but must have been even higher. Cetshwayo's comment on hearing of the price his *impi* had paid for its victory is well known: 'An assegai has been thrust into the belly of the nation ... There are not enough tears to mourn the dead.'

The Flight to the River

There were, however, those who had managed to break through the Zulu encirclement – or more likely had left before the trap had fully closed – and

One of the burial cairns at Isandlwana in the late nineteenth century. (Brown)

these men fled towards the Buffalo River and the imagined safety of the Natal bank. Apart from a few of Zikhali's Horse, who kept their discipline under an Edendale NCO named Simeon Khambula, and even managed to provide covering fire to help their comrades' escape, they were all in complete disorder. Most of them were lightly equipped NNC auxiliaries or mounted men, including those regular officers who had not been attached to the infantry companies and so were not obliged to remain with them. Not a

Looking north-east across the Buffalo River from near the Melvill and Coghill grave site. Although the exact route or routes taken by the fugitives escaping from the disaster at Isandlwana remain debatable, it is likely that many of them came down the hill opposite, or over the shoulder at centre left, which is the route taken by the present-day Fugitives' Trail. Illustrations from the time suggest the slopes were less densely wooded in 1879.

The Buffalo River at Fugitives' Drift, from the southern or Natal side, looking upstream in the direction of Rorke's Drift. The British and their allies who came this way made the crossing from right to left.

single British regular escaped on foot. The Zulu right horn had blocked the obvious way of escape, along the road back to Rorke's Drift, so the fugitives had no choice but to plunge down the steep slope that led southwards to the river crossing that was then known, after the chief who had his *kraal* there, as Sothondose's Drift – nowadays often referred to as Fugitives' Drift. While most of the warriors of the Zulu horns turned towards the camp to finish off the trapped infantry, others took up the pursuit.

The memorial to lieutenants Melvill and Coghill on the hillside overlooking the river on the Natal side. Melvill had succeeded in carrying the Queen's Colours of the 1st/24th as far as the river, where Coghill turned back to help him. The colours were swept away in the river but both officers reached the Natal bank, only to be killed there, apparently by the followers of a local chief called Sothondose, who had been thought to be friendly.

Among the fleeing officers were lieutenants Melvill and Coghill of the 24th. Melvill was carrying the Queen's Colour of the 1st Battalion. The Colour was of enormous symbolic importance to a British battalion, but it was hinted by some commentators that Melvill had taken it to safety as an excuse to leave the battlefield himself. However, this was clearly unfair: as adjutant of the battalion it was his duty to look after the colours, and it is quite likely – though it cannot be proved – that he was ordered to do so by

The grave of lieutenants Melvill and Coghill. The inscription on the base of the cross states: 'This cross was erected over the grave by Sir Bartle Frere in 1879', but this is misleading. In fact Colonel Richard Glyn recorded that he had buried the two officers and put up the cross 'Sir Bartle Frere and staff sent'. On the rear of the cross is the famous inscription 'For Queen and Country Jesu Mercy'.

Colonel Pulleine. In the event he reached the river after a hair-raising ride, but lost his horse and was nearly drowned. Coghill, who was on horseback because of an injured knee, had already got across, but turned back to rescue his friend. The colours were swept away in the current but the two officers succeeded in crossing, only to be killed when they ran into a party of Zulus while climbing the slope on the Natal side. It is said that the killers were not men from Cetshwyo's army but followers of Chief Sothondose, who had previously been friendly to the British but changed sides on seeing the extent of the Zulu victory. The graves of Melvill and Coghill can still be seen near the spot where they fell. The Zulus seem not to have understood the significance of the colours and made no effort to capture them. A couple of weeks later a British patrol found them in the river, and they were restored and later presented to Queen Victoria. Another hero of the retreat was the only Isandlwana participant to receive a VC at the time (Melvill and Coghill were not eligible according to the rules then in force, as they were dead, but they both received posthumous VCs in 1907). This was Private Wassall of the Mounted Infantry, who arrived safely on the Natal bank but then went back to rescue a comrade who had been unhorsed in midstream, calmly tying up his own horse on the Zulu side while he did so.

Chelmsford's Return

Lord Chelmsford had spent the morning skirmishing with small parties of Zulus who were moving across his front, and it was clearly some time before he realised that the Zulu main body was not where he had thought it was. However, he still did not understand that he had been outmanoeuvred, and on the assumption that the enemy was still somewhere in front of him he sent orders back to Pulleine to strike the camp and advance to join him. The order arrived about midday, by which time, as we have seen, it was impossible for Pulleine to obey. But the commander-in-chief had already sent the 1st/3rd NNC, under George Hamilton Browne, back to help pack up the camp, and Browne came within sight of the tents just as the final Zulu attack began. 'I saw in a moment,' he wrote later, 'everything was lost.' Naturally Browne halted his men and sent back a messenger to alert the general.

At about 3 p.m. Chelmsford arrived with his staff to see for himself, but at first he did not believe the reports, furiously accused Browne of lying, and ordered him to continue his march. When they got within about 2½ miles, however, even the commander-in-chief began to realise that something had gone wrong. By this time the fighting was almost over and the victorious Zulus were burning the tents. Chelmsford at last ordered a halt and sent a staff officer to bring up the rest of the column. They finally arrived back at Isandlwana after dark, by which time the Zulus had left, and spent what must have been a dreadful night surrounded by the corpses of their comrades. Before dawn on 23 January they were ordered to march – partly because Chelmsford feared the demoralising effects on his men if they saw what the Zulus had done in the light of day, and partly because he had now received reports that his base at Rorke's Drift had also been destroyed.

ORDERS OF BATTLE, RORKE'S DRIFT, 22–23 JANUARY 1879

The Zulus

Prince Dabulamanzi kaMpande

uThulwana Regiment
uDloko Regiment
iNdlondlo Regiment
iNdluyengwe Regiment

This force basically consisted of the reserve or 'loins' from Isandlwana, minus some of the iNdluyengwe who had stopped to loot the camp. It totalled approximately 4,000 men. Apart from the iNdluyengwe, which shared a *kraal* with uThulwana, all these were older married men, probably in their forties. King Cetshwayo himself had served in the uThulwana, which was the senior and most highly regarded unit in the army, what the British Army would call a 'guard regiment'.

The British

Lieutenant J.R.M. Chard, Royal Engineers

B Company, 2nd Battalion, 24th Foot (Lt G. Bromhead)

One company 2nd/3rd NNC (Captain W. Stevenson)

Stevenson's 'Company' was in fact a collection of 300 or 400 levies who were surplus to requirements and had not been allocated to organised units. All (including their commanding officer) deserted before the battle began.

There was also an assortment of commissariat and transport troops and men from the 1st/24th and other units, some of whom were casualties in the hospital. There are a number of detailed rolls – not always entirely consistent – listing the defenders of Rorke's Drift by name. One of these can be seen in the museum at Isandlwana, while others appear in many of the books on the battle listed in the Bibliography.

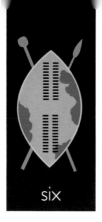

six

The Fight at Rorke's Drift

While the victorious Zulus were looting the camp at Isandlwana and the traumatised survivors were fleeing across the border back into Natal, the second engagement of this remarkable day was about to begin. The commander of the post at Rorke's Drift, Major Spalding, had gone on an errand to Helpmekaar, leaving the engineer officer, Lieutenant John Chard, in temporary command with the famous advice that 'of course nothing will happen'. The distant sound of firing probably reached Rorke's Drift soon after midday, but caused no particular concern. Lord Chelmsford fully intended to bring on an engagement somewhere on the road to Ulundi, and there was no reason at all to suppose that he would lose it. But the Reverend Otto Witt (the missionary whose post this had been before it was requisitioned), Surgeon Reynolds and Chaplain George Smith decided to climb Shiyane – the hill overlooking the post, better known at the time as the Oskarberg – in the hope of seeing what was happening. From the summit the hill of Isandlwana is clearly visible, but most of the fighting was taking place on the far side of the hill, so the three men could not tell which way the battle was going. Soon, however, they could see through a spyglass several bodies of African troops moving in their direction. At first they took them for friendly NNC, until they realised that their mounted officers were also black – obviously not something that one would expect in the British Army of the period. They hurried back to alert Chard, but the alarm had already been raised by a stream of mounted fugitives who were riding past on their way to Helpmekaar.

An attack on Rorke's Drift had not been part of the original Zulu plan. In fact Cetshwayo, still hoping to present himself as the innocent

The view up the Buffalo River in the direction of Rorke's Drift from the Fugitives' Drift road. Somewhere on this stretch Dabulamanzi's regiments crossed the river from the Zulu bank on the right into Natal on their way to attack Rorke's Drift. Again, the country was probably far less densely wooded then.

victim of British aggression, is generally thought to have forbidden his commanders to cross into Natal. But thanks to the speed and completeness of the victory at Isandlwana, the four regiments that had formed the loins had not seen action. They were all veterans, mostly older married men, and were unhappy at missing the opportunity while the youngsters from rival regiments enjoyed all the plunder and glory. Many of their best officers were not present, so their de facto commander was Cetshwayo's half-brother Prince Dabulamanzi, who, although he held no official command,

Looking in the opposite direction from the Fugitives' Drift road just outside the entrance to the lodge property. The heights where Helpmekaar stands can be seen in the distance. Note the ubiquitous aloe bushes, a very characteristic feature of the landscape in this region.

was considered to be the senior officer by virtue of his royal blood. How and why the decision was made is not clear, but Dabulamanzi either ordered an advance on Rorke's Drift, or allowed himself to be persuaded by his impetuous troops. Nevertheless, there may have been more to the move than a desire to 'wash their spears': the post was well known to the Zulus, and no doubt their scouts had confirmed that it was a major British supply base. The Zulus had no arrangements of their own for resupply and the prospect of capturing the stores of gunpowder and above all food

View from the same spot along the road towards Rorke's Drift, with Shiyane Hill on the horizon.

Looking eastwards from the summit of Shiyane. Isandlwana Hill is about 15km away in the distance. This is the view that Otto Witt and his companions would have had in the early afternoon of 22 January.

must have been enticing. Dabulamanzi's force crossed the Buffalo River at two points between Rorke's and Sothondose's Drifts, the iNdluyengwe regiment downstream and the others further west, under the eastern slopes of Shiyane. Neither crossing point was visible from the mission station and the attackers did not come into view until about 4.30 p.m., when they approached around the southern flank of the hill.

By then Chard and Lieutenant Gonville Bromhead, who was in command of B Company of the 2nd/24th Foot but was junior to Chard in the Army List, had had about 90 minutes to make their preparations. The Reverend Smith claimed that Chard and Bromhead's first thought was to load the sick from the hospital into the two wagons they had with them and evacuate the post, though it has been pointed out that Smith would probably have still been scrambling down from Shiyane when this debate took place, so he may

The same view at approximately thirty times magnification. The site of the British camp is hidden behind the shoulder of the hill and the *nek* at centre right. It is obvious that even with a telescope it would not have been possible to see much of the action at Isandlwana from a vantage point on Shiyane.

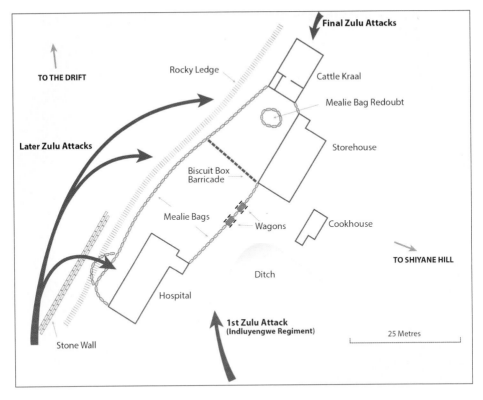

Sketch map of Rorke's Drift as it was in January 1879, showing the improvised defensive lines erected on the afternoon of 22 January.

not have witnessed it himself. According to this account it was an officer of the Commissariat and Transport Corps, Acting Assistant Commissary Dalton, who pointed out that to retreat would be suicide, as British regulars could not hope to outrun Zulus even without the heavily laden wagons, and that their only hope – admittedly a faint one – was to stand their ground. Luckily Chard, as a Royal Engineer, had the skills to create the best possible defence in the time available. Ideally the scrub surrounding the post would have been removed to provide a better field of fire, but there was no time to do this. What he could do was collect mealie bags to make barricades and link the buildings into a continuous defensive position. At this point there were still around 300 NNC troops at the post, and with their help the work of moving the heavy bags was completed just in time. The two wagons were also built into the perimeter between the hospital and the storehouse on the side facing Shiyane. On the opposite side a 'rock step' averaging about 5ft high made a useful natural obstacle, which was enhanced by lining mealie bags along the top of it. At the last moment it was decided to build an additional wall of biscuit boxes across the yard that separated the hospital and the storeroom, running from the north-western corner of the latter to meet the mealie bag barricade on the other side. This was a precaution to allow the men to regroup and make a last stand in case the perimeter was breached. Some accounts describe both Chard and Bromhead as rather dull, uninspiring officers, but it is not clear how much of this was motivated by jealousy among those who had not had their opportunity for glory. Their most often quoted critic was Lord Chelmsford's eventual replacement, Sir Garnet Wolseley, who was unrelentingly critical of just about everything that had happened in Zululand before he took over, and hardly ever had a good word to say for anyone. It would not be surprising either if the events of that day had affected their characters, at least temporarily – post-traumatic stress was not recognised at the time and few contemporaries would have made allowance for its effects. But both officers must have acted decisively to have put the defences in place in such a short time, and the arrangements seem to have met with the approval of most of the military men who have visited the site since.

The battle began as soon as the iNdluyengwe regiment appeared around the corner of Shiyane. By this time B Company and a few individuals from other units were the only defenders left. Half an hour before the attack a party of around 100 Natal Native Horse fleeing from Isandlwana had arrived at the post, led by Lieutenant Henderson, who at first offered his help. Chard asked them to ride back and try to delay the enemy advance, which initially they did, but as soon as they made contact with the enemy they retired on the post, and instead of dismounting to join the garrison, kept riding in the direction of Helpmekaar. Their officer explained to Chard that his men were too demoralised by what they had seen at Isandlwana to obey his orders, but instead of staying to fight he disappeared after them. The NNC troops at the post then climbed over the barricade and followed suit; Bromhead's men were so angry that they actually shot dead one of the white NNC NCOs as he ran. To be fair to the NNC, they had already made a major contribution to the

Approaching the museum building from the entrance to the Rorke's Drift site.
The building post-dates the battle, but was built on the same foundations and gives
a fairly good idea of what the original hospital would have looked like. The original
hospital roof was of thatch, later replaced by iron sheets. The site is roughly rectangular,
with the long axis running from the entrance at the south-western end to the cattle
kraal at the north-east. The defensive positions on this side of the building – usually
referred to as the 'front' of the post – faced north-westwards towards where the car
park is now. The works on the opposite side – the 'rear' – looked towards Shiyane Hill.
Of course, during the battle the post was entirely surrounded, and the terms 'front' and
'rear' were largely irrelevant.

A view of the museum from the front, the direction from which the main Zulu attack was launched. Under the green sign at far left is a 3D model of the Isandlwana–Rorke's Drift area, which is very helpful for understanding the nature of the terrain and its influence on the campaign. Note the steepness of the slope in front of the building. The lines of stones in the grass indicate the location of the British mealie bag defences. An additional semicircular line of defence – just visible in the picture at centre left – was added on the forward slope to strengthen what Lieutenant Chard regarded as the weakest sector of the defences. This did not prevent the Zulus from reaching the building – then the hospital – and eventually capturing it.

Rows of stones in the grass have been placed to show the location of the defensive works erected during the battle at Rorke's Drift.

defence by helping to build the mealie bag walls. They were poorly armed, and could hardly have been usefully deployed on the front line even if they had stayed. At least one of the survivors of Isandlwana did apparently stay to help; this was a Lieutenant Adendorff of the NNC, who was one of the first to bring the news of the disaster and subsequently took up a position inside the storehouse from which, according to Chard, he fought throughout the battle. Unfortunately for him this inconspicuous position meant that most

Looking from the 'rear' of the post, facing away from Shiyane Hill towards the site where the storehouse stood in 1879. To the right of the church the cattle *kraal* is hidden by the sloping ground. The British perimeter on this side ran in a fairly straight line from the storehouse to the hospital, out of shot to the left. Two wagons were incorporated into this section, making it higher and more substantial than the rest of the mealie bag line. It was against this sector that the initial attack by the iNdluyengwe Regiment was made.

of his comrades failed to notice him, and he was later arrested as a deserter from Isandlwana. With Chard's report to vouch for him he escaped a court martial, but the question of whether he was actually at the battle or not remains controversial.

As soon as the men of the iNdluyengwe regiment came within sight of the mission station they deployed into line and launched an attack against the sector of the defences nearest to them, between the two buildings. Today much of the ground over which they attacked has been built up and it is difficult to gain an impression of what it was like, but they had to cross about 500 yards of mainly open ground, exposed to a crossfire from the buildings and the men on the barricade as they got closer. Fifty yards from the perimeter the front ranks of the iNdluyengwe went to ground and returned fire from the cover of a ditch, but the majority of the regiment veered to their left and regrouped in the bushes facing the opposite wall, where the car park is now. Here the vegetation reached almost to the foot of the rock step and the Zulus were able to make use of it to launch their rushes from much closer range. Many of them reached the mealie-bag barricade, only to find that from their elevated position the British were able to repulse them with their bayonets. The Zulus had always relied heavily on their skill at hand-to-hand fighting, but – just as had happened to their colleagues at Isandlwana – they seem to have been shocked to discover that they had met their match in this respect. Several British observers noted that they seemed more wary of the bayonet than of any amount of rifle fire. When Bromhead and B Company's Colour Sergeant Bourne led a detachment of men in a countercharge, the attackers quickly fell back from the barricade.

When the other three Zulu regiments came up, they followed the iNdluyengwe and wheeled around the hospital to deploy at the front of the post. It is not known whether any of these movements were ordered by Prince Dabulamanzi or his *indunas*, or whether they were spontaneous actions on the part of the warriors. Most commentators have found no evidence that Dabulamanzi had a plan at all, but his men – just like those at Isandlwana – were well enough trained in standard Zulu tactical doctrine to make up for the inadequacies at command level. While the bulk of their forces remained concentrated opposite the front wall, others fanned out to

The defence of Rorke's Drift from a
nineteenth-century illustration. (Brown)

surround the post. Several hundred men took their muskets up on to the
slopes of Shiyane, where they found cover among the caves and boulders
below the rocky ledge that ran along that side of the hill, and kept up a steady
fire on the defenders. From there the backs of the British soldiers lining the
front wall were exposed, but the range was too great for the Zulus' weapons
and they were facing into the evening sun, so few casualties were caused.
On the other hand, the defenders on the back wall, firing at the smoke with
their Martini Henrys, killed many of the Zulus. Dabulamanzi is also said
to have taken up a position somewhere on the lower slopes of the hill; this
makes sense as he would have had a good view of the battlefield, though it
is hard to see how he could have issued orders from there to his main body
on the far side of the post.

The attacks kept coming, and eventually the Zulus overran part of the
barricade in front of the hospital, where the ground was more level and the
defences at their weakest. They could not outflank the main line because a
short section of barricade had been built between the north-western corner
of the hospital and the front wall, from where the defenders could catch them
in a crossfire if they attempted to break into the building itself. However,
Chard was becoming worried about the vulnerability of his perimeter,

especially when another rush nearly broke through the front wall in front of the storehouse. Although British casualties had been fairly light, they were beginning to mount up and he had no reserves to replace them. So at about 6 p.m. he ordered a withdrawal behind the biscuit box wall. This was done successfully, though at this point the defenders were probably lucky that the NNC troops had not stayed – there would not have been room for 300 extra

The rocky terrace that runs across the lower slopes of Shiyane Hill, overlooking the rear of the mission station. Zulu snipers kept the defenders under fire from the shelter of these rocks. On top of the terrace at centre right is the mission bell, which is believed to be close to the spot where Prince Dabulamanzi took up his position during the battle.

men inside the new perimeter, and it is easy to imagine that the Zulus might have taken advantage of the inevitable confusion to follow them in. The move kept the men concentrated and took those at the front at least partly out of the line of fire of the Zulus on Shiyane, but it meant abandoning the hospital and its defenders. Almost as seriously, the post's only water supply, which was in a cart in the yard, also had to be left.

Looking towards the Rorke's Drift mission station from the bottom of Shiyane Hill. Access to the hill is through a gate in the fence on this side. The church (the former storeroom) is on the right, and the museum/hospital on the left. The buildings in the foreground are modern.

Looking towards the church from the north-west. Today much of the slope between the car park and the mission buildings, up which the Zulus had to charge, has been graded for easier access, but a section of the original ledge can still be seen on the right of the picture. Visitors are welcome to enter the church, although it should be remembered that it is still a place of worship.

The hospital building was garrisoned by only six able-bodied soldiers, helped by a number of the sick and injured who had been given spare rifles. Jim Rorke had originally built it as a house and storeroom, and it was an extraordinary warren of small rooms, many of them not connected to each other and reachable only from outside. In order to place men in firing positions along the southern and western faces it had been necessary to virtually wall them up in these rooms, blocking the doors with mealie bags and knocking loopholes in the outside walls for them to shoot through. Several rooms had been used as makeshift hospital wards, and there had not even been time to evacuate the sick before the battle began, so that the walking wounded had to take up rifles and join the defenders while their less fit comrades lay helplessly waiting for the Zulus to arrive. Luckily the inside walls were made flimsily of mud bricks, which proved to be a

Another view of the ledge, with the museum building behind. At its highest it is roughly the height of a man.

A close-up of the ledge in front of the church, where the storehouse was situated in 1879. At that time this obstacle ran across most of the position, and was made even more formidable by a wall of mealie bags along the top, behind which stood soldiers with fixed bayonets. From here it can be readily understood why the Zulus, for all their bravery, were unable to take this position by assault.

Looking across the yard from the biscuit-box barricade towards the site of the hospital. Many of the men escaping from the burning hospital got out through a small window in the wall facing the camera, and had to cross the yard illuminated by flames from the burning roof and under fire from Zulus hiding beneath the ledge on which the abandoned section of the front wall stood; part of the line of the wall can just be seen next to the tall tree at far right. Earlier in the battle Surgeon Reynolds had crossed this exposed ground in the opposite direction to carry ammunition to the defenders – one of several brave acts for which he received the VC.

The line of Lieutenant Chard's biscuit-box barricade, running from the front wall to the corner of the storehouse. At centre right is the wall surrounding the small British cemetery. The hospital is out of shot on the right. In front of the camera is the rocky terrace on Shiyane Hill. It is often said that by abandoning the section of the front wall between here and the hospital Chard and Bromhead had eliminated the danger from the Zulus firing from the hill, but from here it can be seen that the men defending the barricade, facing towards the right, could still be enfiladed by fire from that direction.

boon to the defenders because they could easily make tunnels and loopholes through them with picks and bayonets. Although the current building does not preserve the original internal layout, it does give a good impression of the environment in which the subsequent fighting took place. From survivors' accounts it is possible to reconstruct the adventures of some of the individual defenders. These are discussed in several of the books listed under Recommended Reading, though many of the details remain unclear.

The fighting in the hospital lasted for about an hour, between 6.30 and 7.30 p.m., by which time it was getting dark. At some point the Zulus set fire to the thatched roof, probably by throwing spears with bunches of burning grass attached. The thatch was damp and at first burned very slowly, but eventually the defenders realised that they would have to evacuate the building. The rest of Chard's men were now behind the biscuit box wall on the opposite side of the yard, and had in any case been kept busy fighting off incessant Zulu charges, but they were able to give some covering fire to the defenders of the hospital as they tried to break out. The light from the burning roof now proved to be an asset to the defenders. Starting the fire was clearly a mistake on the part of the Zulus, and it seems unlikely that it had been part of Dabulamanzi's plan. Apart from the visibility issue, the Zulus were aware that the mission was a supply base, and could hardly have been certain that gunpowder and ammunition were not being stored in the hospital. The garrison of the building made their escape in various ways. A few ran out into the night and simply lay down among the corpses, where they remained undetected until the next day. Others climbed out of the only window on the side facing the yard, which was 8ft above the ground, dropped into the yard and ran for the safety of the biscuit boxes. Thanks to the covering fire of their comrades behind the boxes most of them made it, including the majority of the sick and injured, though the Zulus now crouching behind what had been the front of the mealie bag barricade threw spears and fired muskets at them. One warrior actually rushed into the yard and speared Trooper Hunter of the Natal Mounted Police, but he was shot dead immediately afterwards, and none of his comrades followed him. The heroic efforts of Private Hook and his comrades in rescuing the patients were to earn them four of the battle's VCs.

Just as it was getting dark, the defenders were heartened by a report that infantry in red coats could be seen coming down the road from

Helpmekaar. At about that time Major Spalding was on his way back with three companions, followed by Major Upcher with D and G Companies of the 2nd/24th, though looking in that direction from the mission station today it is hard to see how anyone could have spotted them. But Spalding met a group of fugitives going the other way, who all assured him that Rorke's Drift had fallen. He climbed a rise beside the road and observed that the hospital was on fire, which seemed to confirm the reports. There were also what seemed to be large bodies of Zulus ahead – though it has been suggested that these might really have been more NNC fugitives – and in the dark the risk of an ambush must have seemed very real. So Spalding and Upcher turned around and marched back to Helpmekaar, unwittingly leaving B Company to its fate.

Chard's new perimeter was easier to defend, but it did have a weak spot, at the corner where the line of biscuit boxes met what had been the front wall between there and the hospital. The rocky ledge that the Zulus had found so hard to assault when the redcoats had been on top it now provided them with cover, from which they could shoot at the defenders at close range. At one point an NNC Corporal named Shiess, despite a serious foot injury, crept out along the wall to dislodge three of these snipers; leaning over the ledge, he shot one of them and bayoneted the others before returning to his position. For this act of bravery Schiess was to be another of the day's VC winners. Also prominent in the defence of this spot was Lieutenant Bromhead, alternately fighting beside his men with a rifle, and leading bayonet charges to disperse groups of Zulus who had managed to get a foothold on the barricades. Chard was clearly not convinced that the perimeter would hold, especially if the enemy managed to set fire to the storehouse roof as well, so he ordered Commissary Dunne to collect the mealie bags that had been left piled in front of the storehouse and make them into a redoubt, hollowed out in the middle, from which a small group of men would make a last stand. Dunne organised this job while under fire from close range. It must have been hard work for the already tired men as well to haul the 200lb bags into position. Today a circle of stones marks the position of this redoubt. It is surprisingly small, and is too close to the wall of the storehouse to have a useful field of fire in that direction, but it was very soon to prove its value.

The front of the church, looking east from the line of the front wall, with the outline of the mealie bag redoubt at left. It was within this small space that the defenders made their last stand.

At the opposite end of the station from the hospital the perimeter included a stone cattle *kraal*, a reconstructed version of which can still be seen. (This is referred to in some accounts as the 'well-built' *kraal*, in contrast to a less substantial enclosure behind it.) The Zulus eventually began to concentrate on breaking in there, where they were not so exposed by the light from the burning roof. In a series of charges they broke in and forced the British to evacuate the *kraal*, but once inside it the warriors were overlooked by the

Looking down on to the mission station from the rock terrace on Shiyane Hill. This view gives an idea of the field of fire available to the Zulu marksmen on the hill, although there were fewer trees in 1879. However, the range is about 350 to 400 yards, which was too far for the Zulus' obsolete muskets to do much damage. On the other hand, the terrace was easily within the effective range of the British soldiers' Martini Henry rifles.

This ring of stones in front of the storehouse marks the position of the redoubt of mealie bags that was constructed under fire as a last-ditch defensive measure.

A closer view of the site of the redoubt. Apart from half a dozen infantrymen firing from inside the redoubt, space was somehow found in the middle to shelter a number of wounded men. It is often remarked that the redoubt must have been larger than the stone markers would suggest, but it is evident from this picture that there was not room to make it much bigger: note how close it is to the wall of the church/storehouse.

soldiers manning Dunne's redoubt, who could shoot down on them from their elevated position protected by the mealie bags. So here too the attack bogged down, and it was in this sector that the last Zulu charges were made, just before 10 p.m. Then both sides resorted to a sporadic exchange of fire that gradually petered out as the night went on. Chard and Bromhead had successfully held Rorke's Drift, although at that time they did not know it.

The well-built cattle *kraal* at the north-eastern end of the post, photographed from the position of the mealie bag redoubt. The last Zulu charges came from this direction after nightfall. It is obvious that from an elevated firing position here the walls provided the attackers with very little cover.

There was one last heroic exploit when Bromhead led a party into the yard to bring in the abandoned water cart, which was successfully done under fire, enabling the defenders – and especially the wounded – to quench their thirst. It is not surprising that both sides were exhausted after several hours of the most brutal close quarters fighting. Even in nineteenth-century warfare prolonged bayonet fighting was very unusual, and the stress as well

The memorial to the defenders who lost their lives in the battle at Rorke's Drift is situated in a small walled enclosure on the south-western side of the site. The names of the dead were carved shortly after the battle by Bandsman Melsop, who had been a stonemason in civilian life. The traditional story has it that he did the job using his bayonet, but the quality of the work makes this seem rather unlikely.

as the physical exertion must have put an almost unbearable strain on the defenders. Firing the Martini Henry over a long period was also hard work, as the notorious recoil became heavier as fouling built up in the barrel. An indication of the ferocity of the battle was the amount of ammunition expended by the men of B Company, who at the end of it had fewer than 1,000 rounds of Martini Henry ammunition left out of a full reserve supply of around 20,000 rounds. This works out at nearly 200 rounds per man over 5 or 6 hours. A soldier was usually sent into battle with seventy rounds in his pouches, and it was very unusual for him to use them all; at the Battle of Khambula in March 1879 the average expenditure of ammunition per

The original memorial to the Zulus who died at Rorke's Drift.

The new memorial to the Zulus at Rorke's Drift is situated behind the ELC Art and Craft Centre. It depicts a leopard on a pile of shields representing the warriors who died there. The leopard has been a powerful symbol in Zulu culture since the time of Shaka, and leopard skins were part of the insignia of high-ranking officers in Cetshwayo's army.

man was thirty-three rounds, while at Ulundi it was only ten. Despite the intensity of the fighting, however, British casualties were astonishingly light – seventeen killed, including two who died later from their wounds, and ten seriously wounded.

For the Zulus, however, things were much worse. First, they had had an approach march of around 15 miles across difficult terrain, then they had attacked straight off the line of march, and kept up their attacks without respite for nearly 6 hours, from 4.30 until 10 p.m. Most of them were middle-aged men only recently mobilised from civilian life, who were unlikely to have been at peak fitness. What was worse, they had little to show for their efforts except for a growing casualty list: the exact Zulu losses are not known, but Chard counted 351 bodies buried by his men after the fight, and there must have been many more whose bodies were retrieved by their friends

This low hill on the opposite side of the road from the mission station to the drift is believed to be the place where a body of Zulus was observed on the morning after the fight at Rorke's Drift. From there they matched away across the river, avoiding Lord Chelmsford's column that was coming from the north to relieve the post.

or who died later from their wounds. Some time in the early hours of the morning they began to withdraw. The next morning Chard saw a body of Zulus appear on a rise opposite the post, but they made no attempt to launch another attack, and soon afterwards Lord Chelmsford's column, coming down from Isandlwana, met Dabulamanzi's force retiring over the Buffalo River. Both sides were too tired and traumatised to face another battle, and in one of the war's more bizarre incidents, they simply marched past each other in opposite directions. At about 8 a.m. on 23 January the British column arrived at the mission station to find to their surprise and relief that the defenders were still holding out around the redoubt and the storehouse. Something, at least, had been salvaged from the day of disaster.

THE RORKE'S DRIFT VCS

The battle at Rorke's Drift is, of course, famous for the highest number of VCs ever awarded for a single day's action – eleven in total. Cynics argue that these awards were politically motivated, with the idea of drawing attention to the only good news for the British in a long string of disasters. Sir Garnet Wolseley, of course, disapproved of them, on the grounds that the post's defenders were trapped and so had no choice but to fight for their lives. Nevertheless, few people are prepared to say who exactly among this company did not deserve a medal for gallantry, and it could just as well be argued that there were men not on the list who also deserved the VC. The following is a very brief account of the medal winners. More details will be found in most books on the subject, and in displays at the Rorke's Drift, Isandlwana and Talana museums. (Rorke's Drift Lodge also sells a collection of eleven bookmarks, each featuring one of the VC winners, which makes a nice memento for anyone interested in the subject.)

Lieutenant John Rouse Merriot Chard, 5th (Field) Company Royal Engineers. Officer commanding in the absence of Major Spalding, the post commander.

As the senior of the two lieutenants he was held mainly responsible for the 'intelligence and tenacity' with which the fight was conducted. Chard's written reports are among the principal sources for the battle. He attained the rank of colonel before dying from cancer in 1897.

Lieutenant Gonville Bromhead, B Company, 2nd/24th Regiment of Foot. With Chard, Bromhead received much of the credit for organising the defence of the post. He also personally fought with great courage, occupying the most exposed position and personally leading several successful bayonet charges. Later Major Bromhead, he died of fever in India in 1891.

Surgeon James Henry Reynolds, Army Medical Department. Reynolds was commended for his gallantry in treating the wounded, and also for single-handedly crossing the yard under fire to resupply the defenders of the hospital with ammunition. He died in 1932, at the age of 88.

Acting Assistant Commissary James Langley Dalton, Commissariat and Transport Corps. Many survivors believed that the successful defence of the post was mainly due to Dalton, who not only supervised the building of the defences – often under fire – but also took an active role in the fighting, saving the life of at least one of his comrades by shooting a Zulu at point-blank range. Reynolds returned to South Africa after his discharge to mine for gold and died there in 1887.

Corporal William Wilson Allen, B Company, 2nd/24th Regiment of Foot. Corporal Allen and Private Hitch maintained communications with the defenders of the hospital despite being exposed to enemy fire from both front and rear, remaining on duty despite being seriously wounded. Promoted to sergeant as a musketry instructor, Allen died in Monmouth in 1890.

Corporal Christian Ferdinand Schiess, NNC. Schiess was of Swiss birth, but is widely regarded as the first South African to win the VC. Although suffering from a badly injured foot, he left the defences to attack a group of Zulus who were shooting from close range, killing three of them before returning to his post to continue the fight despite receiving another wound. Schiess became unemployed after the war and in 1884 he was discovered sick and destitute in Cape Town. He was put on a ship to England but died before it arrived. He was only 28 years old.

Private Frederick Hitch, B Company, 2nd/24th Regiment of Foot. With Corporal Allen, Hitch held a very exposed post under heavy fire, and when seriously wounded continued to help the defence by handing out ammunition. Invalided out of the army, he became a popular London cab driver and died in 1913.

Private Henry Hook, B Company, 2nd/24th Regiment of Foot. The portrayal of Hook as a drunkard and malingerer in the 1966 film *Zulu* is still understandably a cause of resentment among his family and his regiment. In reality he was an exemplary soldier who kept the Zulus in the hospital at bay with his bayonet, enabling himself and Private Williams to bring eight of the patients to safety. Hook left the army in 1880 and later worked at the British Museum. He died in 1905.

Private Robert Jones, B Company, 2nd/24th Regiment of Foot. Both Joneses defended their posts in the hospital with great determination while the patients were evacuated, and both seem to have suffered mental trauma after the confused and desperate fight. Robert Jones committed suicide in 1898.

Private William Jones, B Company, 2nd/24th Regiment of Foot. Private William Jones was invalided out of the army with rheumatism and in later life suffered from mental illness. He died in 1913.

Private John Williams, B Company, 2nd/24th Regiment of Foot. Williams was another of the defenders of the hospital, and with Hook succeeded in bringing eight of the patients to safety. Williams had enlisted under a false name; his real name was Fielding. After the campaign he remained in the army, and later worked at the 24th's regimental depot as a civilian. He died in 1932.

Also prominent in the defence but not awarded the VC was Colour Sergeant Frank Bourne, who is thought to have been the last survivor of the garrison. He was offered a commission, which he initially refused as he lacked a private income, but finished his career as a lieutenant colonel. He was retired by 1914, but volunteered for service in the First World War and served as adjutant to a school of musketry. In 1936 he recorded his account of the battle of Rorke's Drift in a BBC radio broadcast. The recording was destroyed in the 1960s as the BBC apparently thought no one would be interested in the subject (!), but the transcript was published in *The Listener* on 30 December 1936, and Adrian Greaves has reproduced it in his book on the battle. Bourne died aged 91 on VE Day, 8 May 1945.

DID THE ZULUS USE MARTINI HENRYS AT RORKE'S DRIFT?

One of the ongoing controversies surrounding the fight at Rorke's Drift is the question of whether the Zulus deployed captured British Martini Henry rifles against the defenders. That there should be a debate is surprising, given that we have Frank Bourne's categorical statement, made in his 1936 radio broadcast:

> The Zulus had collected the rifles from the men they had killed at Isandlwana ... so our own arms were used against us. In fact, this was the cause of every one of our casualties, killed and wounded ...

On the other hand, most commentators have dismissed this statement, citing three main counterarguments:

First, the Zulu regiments that attacked Rorke's Drift had formed the reserve at Isandlwana and had not actually been engaged, and so would have had no opportunity to capture any rifles.

Second, the Martini Henry bullet used brass rather than paper cartridge cases, which were ejected and discarded when another round was loaded. The former should have survived well, and are often recovered from other battlefields, but none have been found in the places where they might have been expected if the Zulus had fired them, such as the caves along the rock shelf on Shiyane Hill.

Finally, the impact of the .450in-calibre Mark III Boxer bullet fired from the Martini Henry caused characteristically dreadful injuries, as described by Chard from his examination of the Zulu dead after the battle. None of these injuries were found among the defenders' casualties, all of whom had apparently been hit by smoothbore rounds – at least in those cases in which details of their wounds have been recorded.

Each of these assertions, though, can also be challenged in their turn. Dr Adrian Greaves has argued that the Zulu regiments concerned may have overrun an isolated detachment of British troops – from E Company of the 24th Foot, under Lieutenant Dyson – while traversing the Isandlwana battlefield, which could have provided them with perhaps twenty

Martini Henrys. The same author discovered six cartridge cases at a spot further up Shiyane, which might have been dropped by Zulus firing towards the British perimeter. It is also, of course, possible that the Zulus retrieved their used cases instead of discarding them – probably because of the scrap value of the brass rather than with a view to reloading and reusing them, as the cartridge cases used in 1879 were of rather flimsy rolled metal, rather than the solid brass ones introduced later.

Bourne ought to have been familiar with the sound of a Martini Henry being fired, if only because his own unit was equipped with the same weapon. He was clearly wrong, though, to say that all the British casualties were caused by them. Surgeon Reynolds' report identified several men who had been stabbed with assegais, and his colleague Blair-Brown, who treated the surviving men with gunshot wounds a few days later, stated that, 'The wounds were unmistakably made by ordinary round bullets from smooth-bored guns.' On the other hand, the lack of casualties caused by captured rifles does not necessarily mean that the weapons were not used. If there were about twenty of them distributed among 4,000 attackers their impact would have been minimal in any case, but they may even have been less effective in the hands of the Zulus than the obsolete smoothbores. Their users would only have had them for a few hours, and would have had no opportunity to practise with them. The visitor can still stand on the rock shelf on Shiyane and consider how easy it would be to hit a man-sized target in partial cover at that range, especially with a rifle he had never fired before. With unfamiliar sights, a powerful recoil and a flatter trajectory than the muskets to which they were accustomed, it is possible that the captured Martini Henrys consistently overshot their targets and did no harm, while making enough noise to convince even Bourne that they were inflicting considerable damage.

The rocky terrace on Shiyane from immediately below. It was among these boulders and caves that the Zulu marksmen took cover while they fired down on to the defenders of the post.

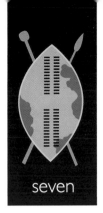

seven

The Aftermath

Rorke's Drift remained a supply base for the rest of the campaign and was never threatened again, though it seems to have been a particularly miserable posting, especially as for some weeks the men were forced to bivouac in the roofless ruin of the hospital. For the Zulus the battle was a defeat that must have detracted somewhat from the victory earlier in the day. David Rattray observed that there seemed to be no real oral tradition about Rorke's Drift

Rorke's Drift as it appeared in the 1890s, from a photograph. (Brown)

RORKE'S DRIFT : AS IT IS TO-DAY.
(From a Photograph by Mr. G. T. Ferneyhough.)

– in stark contrast to Isandlwana. While the latter was understandably celebrated as a great victory, the attack on the mission station was generally dismissed – by those who were not there – as an act of indiscipline by men who had disobeyed their king's orders and deserved to get beaten. In the immediate aftermath of the events of 22 January Chelmsford's column retired across the Buffalo River and orders were sent to the other columns inside Zululand to halt their advance. In the east, near the coast, Colonel Pearson's Number One Column had defeated a Zulu force at Nyezane and occupied an old mission station at Eshowe. On receipt of the new orders he decided to hold the position, but sent back most of his mounted and NNC troops to reduce the strain on his supplies. Their retreat was not carried out in good order and Major Graves, commanding the 2nd NNC, was later involved in a libel case over accusations of cowardice. The Zulus blockaded Pearson at Eshowe but did not try to take the post by assault, and so he was spared a second Rorke's Drift. Meanwhile, Colonel Wood's Number Four Column at the other end of the front was about to attack a Zulu *impi* on top of a flat-topped mountain called Hlobane when Chelmsford's message arrived. Wood called off the attack, though he continued to launch raids against *kraals* in the area. On 12 March came another reverse for the British when a Zulu force attacked a supply column and its escort from the 80th Regiment at Intombe Drift. The column had unwisely halted for the night when halfway across the Intombe River, and the party on the far bank were wiped out in a surprise attack with the loss of around eighty men. The junior officer in command of the remaining soldiers on the other bank, having the only horse, decided to ride off to get help – an action that did further damage to the reputation of the British officer corps when the men he had abandoned were surrounded by Zulus and had to fight their way out under the command of an NCO.

These victories brought only a temporary respite for Cetshwayo. The losses at Isandlwana and Rorke's Drift had been so great that he was no more able than the British to remain on the offensive. In fact, many of his troops had gone home instead of reporting at Ulundi for further orders as they were supposed to do. But by March Chelmsford was beginning to receive reinforcements and was ready to move again. Towards the end of the month, Colonel Wood received orders to create a diversion while Chelmsford advanced to relieve Eshowe. Wood resumed his advance towards Hlobane, but by this time the Zulus had also been reinforced. On 28 March Wood sent his mounted troops and NNC to execute a pincer movement, Lieutenant Colonels Redvers Buller and John Russell climbing the steep slopes of Hlobane from the east and west respectively. Both parties reached the plateau, but then saw the main enemy army approaching and had to descend again in a hurry. Buller's command was ambushed while descending a difficult scree slope at the Devil's Pass and routed with the loss of around 200 men, though Buller himself was awarded the VC for his courage in extricating the survivors. The next day a 20,000-strong Zulu Army attacked Wood's camp at Khambula. It included several regiments that had fought at Isandlwana, including the uKhandempemvu, uMbonambi and iNgobamakhosi, who advanced shouting: 'We are the boys from Isandlwana!' But Wood had fortified the camp and laagered his wagons, and had even had time to set up range markers on the approaches so the defenders knew exactly how to set their sights. The result was that the Zulus were repulsed with around 2,000 dead, while only eighteen British soldiers were killed. The British had learned how to fight the Zulus, and from now on they were to enjoy an almost unbroken run of success.

Lord Chelmsford had deservedly received most of the blame for the disaster at Isandlwana and Sir Garnet Wolseley was soon to be on his way to replace him, but this would take time, and he was anxious to finish the war while he was still in command. On 2 April the relieving army marching towards Eshowe was attacked at Gingindlovu, and this time Chelmsford made no mistakes. Fighting from behind their wagon *laager* the British again defeated a Zulu attack and inflicted enormous losses. The next day Eshowe was relieved. On 21 May a British force reoccupied the battlefield at Isandlwana and began the dispiriting task of burying the dead and clearing up the mess. Then, ten days later, two entire divisions crossed into Zululand to deliver the final blow. There was to be one more disaster for the British on 1 June. The Prince Imperial of France, Louis Bonaparte, who was serving on Chelmsford's staff in an unofficial capacity, was killed when a patrol he was accompanying was ambushed by the Zulus. The young officer detailed to look after him had left the scene in what seemed like unseemly haste, though he had not realised that the prince had been unhorsed and left behind. One more death amid the carnage might not seem all that worthy of note, but the political

In the image on the gravestone:

IN MEMORY
OF
PRIVATE THORNE
6TH. DRAGOONS
WHO WAS DROWNED
IN THE BUFFALO RIVER
BY THE UPSETTING
OF THE PUNT
OCT. 25TH. 1884

There was a British military presence in the area for several years after 1879, and service at Rorke's Drift remained hazardous even without the threat of enemy action. This gravestone, in the same enclosure as the memorial, commemorates Private Thorne of the 6th Dragoons, who drowned in the Buffalo River five years after the battle.

implications were enormous. The dynasty founded by Napoleon Bonaparte had met a sudden and unexpected end. The French were furious, as was Queen Victoria, who was a personal friend of the prince's mother.

By this time Wolseley had arrived in South Africa and was chasing after Chelmsford with the orders appointing him as the new commander-in-chief, but his predecessor managed to stay ahead of him just long enough. On 4 July he approached Cetshwayo's capital at Ulundi and brought the last Zulu Army to battle. There was no opportunity to *laager*, but Chelmsford kept his force concentrated in an enormous square, against which the warriors charged in vain. Some Zulus got within thirty paces of the square before being shot down by Martini Henrys, artillery and Gatling machine guns. Then the British cavalry charged out of the square and turned their defeat into a rout. Ulundi was burnt and Cetshwayo fled. Eleven days later Chelmsford handed over command to Wolseley, but there was nothing left for the latter to do except mopping up. Cetshwayo was captured on 28 August and taken into imprisonment at Cape Town. By September the war was over, and the British Army marched out of Zululand. At first the Zulus retained their nominal independence, but their country was partitioned into thirteen small territories ruled by puppet chiefs, several of whom were renegades who had changed sides when the British victory began to seem inevitable. Fighting soon broke out among the various factions, and in 1881 Cetshwayo visited London and petitioned Queen Victoria for permission to regain his throne. Public opinion had become more sympathetic to the Zulus and the king was greeted by cheering crowds, but thanks to pressure from the authorities in Natal he was restored to only a small rump of his former kingdom. Most ominously his arch rival, Zibhebhu kaMaphitha (who had fought on the Zulu side at Isandlwana), was allowed to keep the lands he had been given in 1879.

Cetshwayo returned in January 1883, but there was soon open war between his followers, known as they had been in 1856 as the uSuthu, and those of Zibhebhu. The uSuthu were defeated in two bloody battles at Msebe and Ulundi, and in February 1884 Cetshwayo died – poisoned, his supporters believed, on Zibhebhu's orders. The uSuthu nevertheless rallied under Cetshwayo's son Dinuzulu, who enlisted the help of the Boers in the Transvaal in exchange for land. These unlikely allies crushed Zibhebhu at the Battle of Tshaneni in June 1884, but the Zulus then found it impossible to get rid of the Boers, who laid claim to most of the country. Zululand was reduced to such misery that the British were forced to return, and in 1887 they annexed the former kingdom, which became part of Natal ten years later. This was the end of Zulu independence, but not the end of the bloodshed. In 1906 a chief named Bambatha led a rebellion against the imposition of a hut tax that was put down by overwhelming firepower, leaving around 4,000 Zulus dead. Dinuzulu had not joined the rebellion, but was suspected of sympathising with it and given a prison sentence for treason.

Nearly ninety years of white domination followed, until the abolition of apartheid and the adoption of a democratic constitution in the 1990s. Today the Zulu people are not badly off by African standards. They are well served by schools and hospitals, and the amount of new building to be seen suggests a certain amount of prosperity. Jobs are scarce in the countryside and many younger people are leaving for the cities, but this is true of most rural areas around the world. Nevertheless, they might justifiably consider that Zululand has not yet recovered from the damage caused by past British policies, not to mention more recent scourges such as the Aids epidemic. The visitor will find opportunities to contribute to a number of charitable causes in

A Zulu in front of his *kraal*, photographed in the 1890s. At this time the appearance of Zulu settlements would have been little changed from twenty years earlier. (Brown)

the area and may well feel that this is an appropriate way of acknowledging these facts.

As for the other main protagonists in the events of 22 January 1879, Lord Chelmsford and his supporters made desperate attempts to pass the blame on to others – notably Colonel Glyn, who was too loyal to fight back; Colonel Durnford, who was conveniently dead; and the NNC. But the government in London was not fooled, and although Chelmsford was 'kicked upstairs' to honourable appointments as Governor of the Tower of London and Colonel of the Life Guards, he was never allowed to command troops in the field again.

Prince Dabulamanzi's career survived his defeat at Rorke's Drift rather better. Although censured by the king for disobeying his orders not to invade Natal or attack fortified positions, he was one of the commanders at the Battle of Gingindhlovu, where he was wounded. He was murdered in 1886 by a Boer after being falsely accused of stock theft. The fate of Ntshingwayo kaMahole, the victor of the day, was in a way even more tragic. He was one of the thirteen puppet chiefs established after the war, but remained loyal to Cetshwayo and was killed by his fellow Zulus when Zibhebhu attacked Ulundi in 1883. Also killed in the same battle was Sihayo kaXongo, whose actions had provided one of the pretexts for the British invasion.

THE LANDSCAPE OF OLD ZULULAND

The battlefields region today is a farmed landscape, divided by wire fences and dotted with villages and isolated buildings, not quite the 'wild Africa' that some visitors expect – though the valley of the Buffalo River below Rorke's Drift is still forested and gives a good impression of wildness. Most of the buildings are of modern design, and although you will see a few of the traditional round thatched huts or *rondavels*, few Zulus now live in them permanently. On the whole the typical combination of grassy pasture on the level areas and thorny scrub on the steeper and more broken ground gives a fair general indication of the terrain and vegetation as they were in 1879, but there have inevitably been some changes. The Buffalo River marks the boundary between what was the old British province of Natal and Zululand proper, and the difference between the two is apparent on the ground even today. The Natal side, where Rorke's Drift itself is situated, is divided into plots of private land, mostly farms dedicated to raising livestock, and is more densely forested and fenced. On the Isandlwana side, although the main land use is still cattle raising, the land is controlled by the Zulu communities rather than by private farmers, and the country is less fenced and more open, with long lines of sight to the surrounding mountains, just as it was at the time of the battles. As in most of South Africa, though, barbed-wire fences make wandering at random across the countryside impractical.

Of the two types of acacia or thorn bush that are prominent in the area, only the flat-topped species with greyish green leaves is indigenous. The darker, round-topped variety was introduced by Boer farmers and had probably not arrived in the area in 1879. Even today the latter are less common in Zululand than on the Natal side of the river, and efforts are under way to eradicate them as an invasive species. The eucalyptus plantations are, of course, also modern introductions, as are the jacarandas whose lilac flowers enliven the countryside in the spring. However, the tall, spiny aloes are native, and nineteenth-century drawings show they were as prominent a feature of the landscape then as they are now.

A view of the terrain on the lower slopes of Shiyane Hill. Most of the steep and rocky ground in the area is dotted with these thorn and aloe bushes, which contemporary illustrations show were equally abundant at the time of the Anglo-Zulu War. They are not dense enough to block lines of sight or impede the movements of skirmishing troops, but would obviously be an obstacle to the manoeuvres of formed bodies.

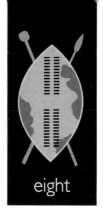

eight

Getting There

South Africa is a well-established tourist destination and getting there presents no particular problems. There are no compulsory vaccinations, though diphtheria, tetanus, hepatitis A and polio are usually recommended. Malaria prophylaxis is not required in Kwazulu-Natal, unless you plan to stay overnight in a few of the lowland game reserves. Medical services are generally good – there is a brand-new hospital in Nqutu, about 25km from the battlefields – but they can be expensive, so you should make sure you have adequate travel insurance. Citizens of the EU, the USA, Canada, Australia and New Zealand do not need visas. However, you will need to have at least one completely empty page in your passport to be stamped with a visitor's permit, which is valid for ninety days. Currency is the rand, which is easily obtainable outside the country. At the time of writing the sterling exchange rate was about £1 to 18 rand. Large establishments will take debit or credit cards, but you will certainly need cash at some point, even if you are on an organised tour, if only for tipping guides and hotel staff. Most guidebooks will advise you that ATMs are available everywhere, but this is not the case in the battlefields region, where you might easily find yourself 50km from the nearest machine.

The battlefields can be visited at any time of year. The rainy season coincides with the Southern Hemisphere summer, and usually peaks in January around the anniversary of the battles of Isandlwana and Rorke's Drift. If you want to see the country as it was at the start of the 1879 campaign, with the grass high and the rivers full, this is the obvious time to visit. It is also the hottest time of year and can be uncomfortably humid, but although you need to be prepared for heavy downpours it does not usually rain all the time and the roads are still passable. The rest of the year the climate is fairly temperate, and the most popular tourist season is in the spring, around October. The area can be surprisingly cold even at that time of year, and as the amount of cloud cover can vary dramatically from day to day, so can the temperatures. The lodges

A distant view of the Mangeni Hills from the site of the camp at Isandlwana. Note the low cloud and poor visibility: the visitor should be prepared for such conditions even in the southern spring.

find it necessary to provide electric blankets for chilly nights. Remember that the average altitude of the region is around 1,000m. It is therefore difficult to advise on what clothing to take; you will certainly need a good hat and a supply of sunscreen, but a warm windproof jacket may be just as useful.

Organised coach tours generally begin and end in Johannesburg, but the nearest major city to Rorke's Drift, and the most convenient arrival point and touring base if you are travelling independently, is Durban. Most international airlines fly into Johannesburg, but several companies operate connecting flights to Durban. At present the only international routes to use Durban's King Shaka International Airport are operated by Emirates from Dubai and by Ethiopian Airlines from Addis Ababa, but both are served by frequent connections from Europe. Durban airport is 35km north of the city and a taxi ride could prove expensive, but a fairly regular shuttle minibus service runs from outside the airport's main entrance to the city centre. This tends to leave when it is full rather than at the scheduled times, and the trip can take anything up to 2 hours depending on traffic, but the driver will drop you off at your hotel on request. Plenty of very reasonably priced accommodation can be found along the seafront in Durban; at the time of writing the North Beach area is said to be safer than the South Beach, but tourists in this area do need to take the usual precautions against crime. Most visitors will want to spend several days in the battlefields region, but for those who are short of time it is possible to book day trips to Rorke's Drift and Isandlwana with several operators in Durban. From personal experience I can recommend First Zulu Safaris (Ushaka Marine World, phone +0027 (31) 3373103, www.1stzulusafaris.co.za), though I have not taken this particular tour.

Rail and bus services run between Johannesburg and Durban, but at present go no closer to the battlefields region than Ladysmith. There is no public transport infrastructure elsewhere in the region, and so for those who are not travelling with an organised coach tour the only realistic option is to hire a car, either self-drive or with a driver. There are transit companies in each of the major cities that will drive you to Rorke's Drift at a fairly reasonable cost – at the time of writing about R2,500 to R3,000 for a one-way trip from Durban (which is not unreasonable bearing in mind that this involves a return journey for the driver totalling around 8 hours).

Sunrise over the waterfront in Durban. The city is the most convenient base for a visit to the Zulu War battlefields; from Durban to Rorke's Drift is a four-hour journey by car.

The driver might ask you to pay for fuel, but the cost should be deducted from your bill at the end of the trip. Fuel is relatively cheap in South Africa, currently about 60 per cent of the price in the UK. Most major routes, including the N2 and N3, are toll roads, but will accept cards if you do not have cash.

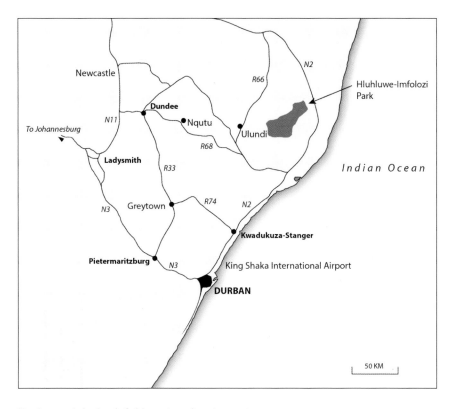

Durban and the battlefields region, showing major routes.

By road there are three possible routes from Durban to Rorke's Drift, each taking around 4 hours. One follows the N3 from Durban via Pietermaritzburg, then the N11 through Ladysmith. About 26km beyond Ladysmith turn right on the R602 to Dundee. At Dundee follow the R68 towards Nqutu, then turn right just before Nqutu on to a dirt road signposted to Rorke's Drift Lodge. The distance from here is about 23km. Isandlwana is reached via another dirt road on the left, just before you reach Rorke's Drift, where the battle site is also signposted on the left. This route takes the best roads, but this is offset by the greater distance, so there will not be much saving in time. It is, however, recommended if you have an interest in the battlefields of the Second Anglo–Boer War; Ladysmith and Talana are on the route, while Elandslaagte and Spioenkop (Spion Kop) are nearby, and are well signposted. Going this way will also provide some good views of the Drakensberg Mountains to the north and west.

Alternatively, leave the N3 at Pietermaritzburg and take the R33 north to Greytown. Continuing through Greytown on the same road you pass through the little towns of Keat's Drift, Thukela Ferry and Pomeroy. There are occasionally some problems with this road and it would be wise to check in advance that it is open. The terrain on the route is hilly and the going is relatively slow, though the road is well surfaced, but its great attraction for Anglo-Zulu War aficionados is that it follows the principal route taken by the

Looking west over the Talana battle site and the town of Dundee towards the outliers of the Drakensberg Mountains. Dundee is the nearest large town to the Isandlwana and Rorke's Drift battlefields, and is an excellent base for touring the region.

Sign on the track to Rorke's Drift Lodge. The 'Authentic African Experience' refers to the unsurfaced road, which has gained some notoriety with visitors. In fact, it is not bad by African standards and does not require a four-wheel drive vehicle, at least when it is dry. It is bumpy, though, and you do need reasonable ground clearance; trying it in a Ferrari is not recommended! The lodge dogs are not a problem, but there are Anatolian sheep dogs guarding the sheep along the track. These will leave you alone as long as you are not perceived to be a threat to the sheep, but if on foot it is a good idea to be aware of them and give them plenty of space. Unfortunately they are the same size and colour as the sheep, though they stand out even at a distance when they move.

British troops marching from Durban to the front in 1879. It does not require much imagination to get an impression of what they had to endure: much of the terrain in this central section is steep and thickly strewn with boulders, and even today it does not seem capable of supporting more than a few goats, in stark contrast to the open pastures of Zululand further on. About 10km beyond Pomeroy turn right on to a dirt road signposted Elandskraal, then follow the road through a sharp left turn until you arrive at the little settlement of Elandskraal, easily recognised by its eye-catching church. Just beyond the church is a left turn signposted Rorke's Drift. The turning to Fugitives' Drift Lodge is about 7km along this road on the right. Rorke's Drift itself is 7km further on, and you will approach it from the opposite direction to the first route; the battlefield is signposted on the right, just past the sign to Rorke's Drift Lodge on the left.

The third option is recommended if you are driving direct from King Shaka International Airport. Instead of taking the N2 south to Durban, go north to kwaDukuza-Stanger (often referred to simply as Stanger) and take the R74 via Kranskop to Greytown. Then turn right on to the R33 and follow the directions given above.

Health and Security

Most of the time no special precautions are necessary when walking around the battlefields. Snakes are present, including venomous varieties such as the puff adder and the Mozambique spitting cobra, but these are seldom encountered. The more noise you make when walking the safer you are, as snakes will actively avoid people if they can. Needless to say, going barefoot is not recommended. As in most warm regions of the world, it is also a good idea to stay out of caves in case of scorpions. Large centipedes and big hairy 'baboon spiders' might occasionally be seen, but the risk of being bitten is slim unless you try to pick one up. If you were bitten you would be well advised to keep calm and seek immediate medical attention. Most snakes are not venomous, and those that are do not often inject a lethal dose, while traditional remedies such as alcohol or tourniquets can do more harm than good. The risk of attack by large wild animals is completely negligible, though there are white rhinos at the Spioenkop battle site; these are much less aggressive than the rarer black rhino, but visitors are nevertheless advised to give them a wide berth.

Small children should, of course, be instructed never to pick up or touch any kind of animal without checking with an adult first. This also goes for the local dogs. On some farms in Natal the sheep are guarded by large Anatolian sheep dogs; these have a reputation for aggressiveness and should not be approached, but as long as you act calmly and give 'their' flocks as wide a berth as possible the risk of trouble is very low. The Zulu cattle will sometimes be found wandering on the roads and drivers do need to be aware of them, but although the big bulls look formidable they do not seem to be aggressive. Ticks might be encountered if walking through long grass in the wet season (the southern summer), and it would be advisable to wear socks and long trousers for protection as their bites can carry diseases. For most of the year, however, the vegetation will be too sparse for them to present a problem. There are, of course, mosquitoes; in this area they do not carry malaria, and they are not as numerous as in many other parts of Africa, but their bites can still be an annoyance. It is sensible to cover arms and legs after dark if this becomes an issue. If you are walking away from the managed battle sites themselves, you are certain to collect some scratches from thorn bushes and particularly the ubiquitous aloes, whose leaves are edged with needle-sharp spines, but these are minor irritations and usually heal quickly.

A bigger concern in South Africa generally is crime, but the battlefields region is relatively safe. The local people are accustomed to visitors and are almost without exception very welcoming. Any problems encountered are less likely to be when walking the battlefields than when in transit on the roads. Local advice is to lock car doors when driving, and to take particular care at night at choke points such as the stop signs on single-track bridges, where vehicles may have to stop or slow down to wait for oncoming traffic. If you feel that a situation is threatening it is probably best to ignore road signs and keep moving; I am assured that the police will take such circumstances into consideration! You may hear stories about farmers in remote areas being the victims of violence, but on examination most of these incidents turn out to be the outcome of local circumstances and have no implications for the safety of visitors. A lot of publicity has recently been given to 'xenophobic' attacks on foreigners in Kwazulu-Natal, but this is aimed at migrants from other African countries who are perceived as running criminal gangs, dealing drugs and threatening local jobs, and tourists are not likely to be affected. It is, in any case, mainly a phenomenon of the larger cities.

Local Accommodation

Battlefield tourism is an important business in the area, and standards of accommodation are very high. While there are plenty of good places to stay in Ladysmith, Dundee and further afield, the visitor who wants to spend

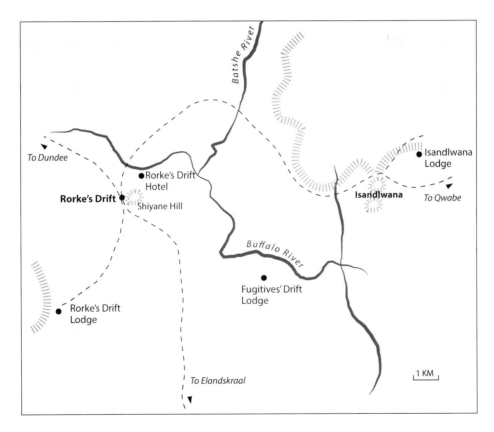

The Rorke's Drift–Isandlwana area as it is today.

several days touring the battlefields will probably find it more convenient to stay in one of the establishments in the immediate vicinity. These are all designed to cater for the aficionado of the Anglo-Zulu War battles, and all can arrange tours with knowledgeable guides. Contact details are:

Fugitives' Drift Lodge: www.fugitivesdrift.com
email: reservations@fugitivesdrift.com

Isandlwana Lodge www.isandlwana.co.za
email: lodge@isandlwana.co.za

Rorke's Drift Hotel www.rorkesdrifthotel.com
email: info@rorkesdrifthotel.com

Rorke's Drift Lodge www.rorkesdriftlodge.com
email: reservations@rorkesdriftlodge.com

Isibindi Zulu Lodge
email: res@isibindi.co.za

Without having personal experience of all of them it is difficult to make recommendations, but Fugitives' Drift and Isandlwana Lodge represent the top end as far as luxury is concerned, and both are situated in locations of great historical interest. The grounds of the former include both the drift itself and the graves of lieutenants Melvill and Coghill, while Isandlwana Lodge is built into the ridge north of Isandlwana Hill and actually overlooks the battlefield. (Those who feel that this might be rather intrusive need not worry: it is not the nearest building to the battlefield and has been carefully designed to be inconspicuous from a distance.) Rorke's Drift Hotel is a relatively new establishment and is situated on the flat land between the slopes of Shiyane and the Buffalo River, within an easy stroll of the mission station. Isibindi Lodge is slightly further away than the others, about 8km from Rorke's Drift on the road to Elandskraal, but has its own game reserve with a wide variety of wildlife.

The battlefields region is as rich in bird life as it is in history. Common species include this exotic-looking masked weaver, photographed here in the grounds of Rorke's Drift Lodge.

In my opinion the best choice for those on a budget, and especially those travelling with families, would be Rorke's Drift Lodge. It is a little more secluded than the others, being at the end of a 5km track that starts across the road from the mission station itself. This track is bumpy and steep in places and has received some bad publicity, but it is perfectly possible to traverse it in an ordinary car, though you should contact the lodge for advice if the weather is very wet. The Rorke's Drift battle site can be reached from here by a pleasant walk of an hour or so. You will need transport to get to Isandlwana, but tours can be arranged through the lodge. It is even possible to visit Isandlwana from here on horseback, though this is an all-day trip that is recommended only for experienced riders. The place itself is in a quiet rural setting on the lower slopes of the Biggarsberg Mountains and comprises four separate lodges, all with spectacular views across Zululand. It is officially self-catering and cooking facilities are provided, but excellent meals can be served in the lodges if required, though you should order these in advance of your visit as there are no shops locally and supplies cannot easily be obtained at short notice. The lodge is famous for its bird life and there are several walking routes around the extensive grounds.

Tours and Guides

If you are staying at one of the local lodges you will no doubt want to take advantage of their organised guided tours of the battlefields. It is, of course, possible to do it yourself with the aid of a guidebook such as this one, but if you really want to get the most out of your visit it is a good idea to employ a professional guide. There is now a rising generation of Zulu guides, who can offer a slightly different perspective on events. I can recommend Thulani Khuzwayo, who is based at Rorke's Drift and can be contacted via Rorke's Drift Lodge. Thulani has a personal as well as a professional interest in the Anglo-Zulu War as one of his ancestors fought with the uKhandempemvu regiment at Isandlwana; he survived the battle unscathed, only to be killed six months later attacking the British square at Ulundi.

A more expensive but more convenient alternative is to book a package tour that includes travel to South Africa, coach transport, accommodation and guides. These can often be tailored to the visitor's specific requirements, and enable you to see places that are not easily accessible on your own. Among the companies that organise such tours from the UK is The Cultural Experience (info@theculturalexperience.com), whose guides include the prolific Zulu War author Ian Knight.

Local landowners are attempting to restore some of the area's wildlife, partly with an eye to the tourist industry. This bontebok near the memorial to lieutenants Melvill and Coghill at Fugitives' Drift is a recent reintroduction to a region in which most of its wild ancestors had already been wiped out by 1879.

GAME AND BIRD WATCHING

Many visitors will want to combine a battlefield tour with a glimpse of South Africa's famous wildlife. The large wild mammals had already been mostly exterminated in the region a decade or so before the Anglo-Zulu War, but in recent years private landowners have begun to encourage or even reintroduce some of them as tourist attractions, so that it is quite likely that there is more big game there now than there was in 1879. The best place to see it is in the grounds of the lodges, where the animals are protected and fairly used to humans. Isibindi Lodge has a particularly wide variety of species. There are blesbok, zebra and giraffes at Fugitive's Drift, while Rorke's Drift Lodge has kudu, impala and even a rather elusive leopard.

For the 'Big Five', however, the best place to go in Kwazulu-Natal is the Hluhluwe-Imfolozi Game Reserve east of Ulundi. This was once the hunting preserve of the Zulu king Shaka, and although small by African standards it retains the air of a genuine piece of wilderness – at least as long as the local people continue to resist the proposed development of an enormous coal mine just outside the perimeter fence. As well as high densities of elephants, lions, buffaloes and other game, it is the best place in the world to see wild rhinoceros; in fact it is the only place where you can see genuinely indigenous white rhinos. A small population of this extraordinary animal was rediscovered here after it was believed to have been driven to extinction in the 1890s and all the specimens in other parks are reintroductions descended from those survivors. The battle against poachers continues to this day. At the Umfolozi entrance gate is a memorial that will dispel any notion that wildlife preservation is just the province of hippies and tree-huggers. It contains a long list of the names of those who have died here in the cause of conservation – mostly killed either by poachers or, ironically, by the animals that they were trying to protect. The reserve can be reached in about 3 hours from Durban via the N2 coast road, and several companies including 1st Zulu Safaris organise day trips by minibus. Alternatively, the reserve is accessible to private vehicles, but you should take care only to leave your vehicle at designated viewpoints and to allow plenty of time to leave before dark. If the park authorities find you in the reserve at night without permission you face a heavy fine – although, of course, in a place that is home to around 100 lions this is not necessarily the worst that can happen!

The battlefields area is also a popular venue for bird watchers. Rorke's Drift Lodge, for example, claims an impressive total of 120 species seen in the grounds, including such rare and spectacular sights as the turkey-sized ground hornbill.

Hluhluwe-Imfolozi is the oldest game reserve in Africa and was once the hunting preserve of the Zulu kings. It covers a relatively small area but offers some excellent game viewing and is said to be home to the densest concentration of wild rhinos in the world.

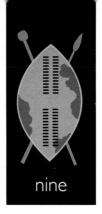

nine

A Visit to Isandlwana

As most of the lodges in the vicinity are closer to Rorke's Drift and the road to Isandlwana passes close by the settlement there, most visitors will probably visit Rorke's Drift first. This, however, is not necessarily ideal, because the battle at Isandlwana took place earlier in the day, and events there influenced what was to happen later at the mission station. We will therefore look first at the Isandlwana battlefield, though noting that it will sometimes be necessary to do the tour in the reverse order. Occasionally, energetic visitors walk from Rorke's Drift to Isandlwana, which takes about 3½ hours each way, but this will not leave much time to look around. The dirt road to Isandlwana is well signposted on the right as you leave Rorke's Drift in the direction of Dundee. It takes you across the Buffalo River by a modern bridge, then east for about 18km on the Zululand side of the river. About 5km beyond the river the road crosses the Batshe River, and a good view can be obtained from here of the lower part of the Batshe Valley, the site of the engagement of 12 January, though Sihayo's *kraal* itself is out of sight behind a spur of the ridge on the eastern side of the valley.

The road approaches the Isandlwana battle site via a route north of the distinctive hill that has given the battle its name, unlike the track in use in 1879 that crossed the *nek* on the southern side. On the way you will pass several gullies in the hillside on your left, down which the regiments of

The first stop for most visitors will be the mission station at Isandlwana, which now incorporates a small visitor centre and museum where admission tickets for the battlefield park itself must be purchased.

the Zulu right horn advanced to surround the British camp. The entrance to the battlefield is beyond the mission station, on the far side of the hill. Isandlwana Lodge is built into the ridge on your left. The area is considerably more densely populated than it was at the time of the battle, and an extensive settlement now lies between the edge of the Nqutu Plateau and the hill itself. There is a small museum and visitor centre in the mission building.

This is currently open from 8 a.m. to 4 p.m., Mondays to Fridays, and 9 a.m. to 4 p.m. at weekends. It has a small collection of artefacts found on the battlefield, and some interpretation boards written in isiZulu and English. There is also a brief account of the battle written by Julian Whybra, and a roll listing the British participants in the events of 22 January, including the defenders of Rorke's Drift.

The road that runs up on to the Nqutu Plateau provides excellent views of the entire Isandlwana battlefield as far as the Mangeni Hills. Isandlwana Hill is just out of shot to the right.

The lip of the Nqutu Plateau, where the British pickets were sited, can be reached on foot or by car via a side road on the left, just behind the mission station. There are excellent views down towards Isandlwana Hill from several points along the top, and it must be said that from here it is difficult to fault the disposition of the British camp itself. Isandlwana is a useful landmark, but it is nowhere near big enough to conceal the approach of an enemy from

Much of the area surrounding the battlefield park, where the initial engagements of the battle took place, is occupied by farms and settlements. Parts of it can be traversed on foot, but it is best to explore it with the assistance of a guide.

any direction, except possibly the unlikely one along the Rorke's Drift road. The Zulus could – and did – approach under cover of the numerous small ridges and gullies on the plateau you are standing on, but the crest is too far from the camp for it to be threatened from there by any weapons available to Cetshwayo's army. Looking in the opposite direction, away from Isandlwana, however, illustrates another problem with Pulleine's deployment. It is not easy to find a position that gives a good line of sight

The entrance to the battle site at Isandlwana. This and Rorke's Drift are the only places in the country where the South African and British flags can be seen flying side by side, a tribute to the men of both sides who fought and died here.

across the plateau to the north. Troops deployed up here, therefore, could be said to have had the worst of both worlds; too far away from the camp to be properly supported, but without any corresponding advantage in the form of an improved field of fire. It is possible to visit some of the places on the plateau where the Zulu Army is thought to have formed up before the battle, but the distances are considerable and this is best attempted with the assistance of a guide.

Looking east across the plain from the road leading to the car park at the Isandlwana battle site. The car park is situated on the *nek* between Isandlwana Hill and the feature to the south known as Mahlabamkhosi, approximately where the British wagons were parked during the battle.

Descending from the plateau again by the way you came, turn left on to the road at the bottom and follow it around the hill to the entrance to the battlefield proper. The enclosed battle park is marked by the South African and British flags flying side by side and covers a relatively small area corresponding roughly to the British camp and the last stand. The car park is on the far side, south of Isandlwana Hill, on the *nek* between it and the hill opposite. This latter feature is Mahlabamkhosi, known to the British at the time as the 'stony koppie'. It was in this vicinity that the British wagons were parked. The site is dotted with whitewashed stone cairns marking the places where British and colonial soldiers are buried, though these are not necessarily on the exact spots where they died. One of the few individually marked graves is that of George Shepstone, the son of Theophilus Shepstone, who was serving on Durnford's staff and had been sent to reconnoitre the heights to the north. He had galloped back to the camp to warn Colonel Pulleine of the approach of the Zulus and had remained to fight alongside its defenders. Immediately above the car park, high on the side of the hill, is an isolated cairn that can be reached by a faint track. It was probably down the slope here that Lieutenant Younghusband led the survivors of his C Company in their last suicidal charge. On the plain below are stone memorials to the dead of the 24th Foot and the various units of the colonial troops. Especially worthy of note is the memorial to the Zulu dead, erected as recently as 1999, which is near the north-eastern perimeter of the site, on the left of the road as you enter. It is in the form of a necklace made of *iziqu* beads, of a type that was traditionally awarded only to those members of the first unit to break the enemy line who had also themselves killed an enemy. After Isandlwana this honour was awarded by King Cetshwayo to the uMbonambi regiment, whose warriors claimed to have been the first to enter the British camp. Adjacent to the memorial is a small buffalo thorn tree, which also has a special significance in Zulu tradition (see page 156).

Three other features are outside the official battlefield but can be reached on foot across the plain to the east. Independent travellers seldom visit them and using a guide would be advisable to get the best out of the sites, but details of a walking trail can be obtained from the visitor centre. Before it was driven back towards the camp by the advance of the Zulu chest, the British firing line ran along the low ridge about 500m north-east of the camp.

The memorial to the Zulu dead at Isandlwana, designed by Gert Swart and erected in 1999. It is in the form of an *isiqu* necklace, traditionally the highest Zulu award for bravery. It also incorporates four bronze head rests, symbolising the spirits of the warriors now at rest.

It appears that the men were drawn up on the forward, or north-eastern, slope of this ridge, as from the other side they would have had no line of sight to the Zulus advancing from the bottom of the escarpment. Archaeologists have discovered spent Martini Henry cartridges in this area, which tends to confirm this view. The memorial to the men of the Royal Artillery

151

is in the same direction, approximately on the spot where Major Smith's battery was overwhelmed. It is less than a metre high and not easy to find without a guide, especially if the grass is long. The ravine, or *donga*, where Colonel Durnford had his final position before retiring into the camp is about 700 metres beyond the camp to the east, and is marked by a group of buildings clustered around a modern clinic. Bear in mind that the terrain here is seriously affected by erosion due to the sporadic heavy rains, and it is likely that most of the *dongas* – including this one – are now wider and deeper than they were in 1879. At the time of the battle this one must have been shallow enough for men standing on the bottom to see and shoot over the eastern lip.

Looking towards Isandlwana across the *nek* from a position near the base of Mahlabamkhosi.

Looking eastwards down the valley some of the more distant features of the area of operations can be easily seen, such as the 'notch' over which the regiments of the Zulu chest came down from the plateau, the conical hill known as Amatutshane behind which the left horn came, and the line of the Mangeni Hills in the distance where Lord Chelmsford was when the battle took place. From here it would seem to be impossible for the main Zulu Army to have moved across the valley from south-east to north-west in order to take up its position on the plateau without being observed from the camp. There is, however, extensive dead ground in that direction, the existence of which is not obvious from a distance. The best way to understand it is to look at the three-dimensional terrain model outside the museum at Rorke's Drift.

Fugitives' Drift and the Fugitives' Trail

Guided walks down the Fugitives' Trail that leads from the *nek* at Isandlwana down to the Buffalo River can be arranged, but this can only be done on an organised tour. The graves of lieutenants Melvill and Coghill overlooking Fugitives' Drift are on private land belonging to Fugitives' Drift Lodge, but access to the site from the Natal side is permitted to non-residents, though you should keep to the road or path at all times. The road to Fugitives' Drift is signposted off the road between Rorke's Drift and Elandskraal. At the top of the hill there is a gate giving access to the property, where you should report to security for permission to proceed. From here, incidentally, there is a good view back down the road towards Shiyane, with the Helpmekaar heights on your left and the valley of the Buffalo River on the right. Once through the gate follow the road for a short distance, with the lodge itself on your right, until you reach a small parking area overlooking the river. The memorial and the graves of the two officers are a short climb up the hill on your left. This is a well-visited spot and fresh flowers are still regularly left here. There is also a buffalo thorn tree and a small cairn in memory of the Zulu 'unknown soldiers' who died in the vicinity. From the memorial there is a good view of the drift itself and the slopes on the far side of the river, down which the survivors from Isandlwana made their escape. To judge from contemporary illustrations the slopes were less well wooded in 1879 than they are now, but

This small whitewashed cairn next to the Melvill and Coghill grave site commemorates an unknown Zulu casualty, and it appears that the local people still add stones to it from time to time (as did I in October 2015). A buffalo thorn tree is growing close by, but it is not clear whether it was deliberately planted or has grown there naturally.

in January the river would be much higher and faster flowing than it is for most of the year. If you want to see more of this area you should enquire at Fugitives' Drift Lodge. There are occasional organised events such as horse rides and even races down from Isandlwana to the river, which might give a flavour of what the fleeing soldiers endured.

Looking down the Buffalo River to the east from near the Melvill and Coghill memorial. The white car at right indicates the position of the access road via Fugitives' Drift Lodge. Although this is private land, visitors are permitted to drive to this point and climb the hill to the grave site. From here a good impression can be obtained of the sort of terrain that the fugitives escaping from the battle had to cross.

THE BUFFALO THORN TREE

The 'buffalo thorn', *Ziziphus mucronata*, is a common native tree in the region, but its regular occurrence near to the battle sites of the Zulu War is no coincidence. It has a special spiritual significance in Zulu culture and it was once the custom to plant one of these trees on the site where a Zulu died away from home. Planted specimens protected by wire fences form part of the Zulu war memorials at both Isandlwana and Rorke's Drift. There is a similar thorn tree near to the cairns at the Melvill and Coghill grave site at Fugitives' Drift, but it is not known whether it was planted deliberately or has simply grown there by chance.

This buffalo thorn tree has been planted next to the new memorial to the Zulu dead at Isandlwana. These trees are of great spiritual significance to the Zulus, and are traditionally planted wherever a Zulu dies away from home.

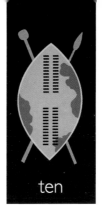

ten

A Visit to Rorke's Drift

The Rorke's Drift battle site is on the right of the road if approaching it from Elandskraal. It is on private land, owned by the Lutheran Church community, but is leased and managed by the Provincial Monument Council. There is a small charge for admission, and the site is open from 9 a.m. to 4 p.m. Go through the gateway marked 'Shiyane Rorke's Drift' and follow the road into the car park on the left. On your left is the small building where you pay for your tickets. On the right near the entrance is another modern building housing the ELC Art and Craft centre, toilets and a small shop where you can buy refreshments. The shop is not always staffed at quiet times, but there should always be someone in the craft centre who will help you. There are also rooms at the rear reserved for various educational activities. As you stand facing this building, the battle site proper is on your left. It may be advisable at this point to clear up an issue that is still sometimes raised by unsuspecting visitors. The location in no way resembles that of the film *Zulu*, because the film was not shot here. Instead, a far more spectacular setting was chosen in the Royal Natal National Park in the Drakensberg Mountains, about 160km to the west. (If you are interested in the film and its sometimes tenuous relationship to reality, try P. Raby *Zulu: The Truth Behind the Film* (York: Paul Raby, 2009).) While on the subject, it is interesting to note that a sequence in the 1979 film *Zulu Dawn* does feature the area of

As at Isandlwana, the British and South African flags mark the Rorke's Drift battle site.

Rorke's Drift. The film's subject is the Battle of Isandlwana, but the presence of the cairns and memorials on that site obviously made it unsuitable for filming. However, the scene showing the British column crossing the Buffalo River was filmed at the actual drift, though with the British going the wrong way, from Zululand to the Natal side. This was clearly done for cinematic reasons, as the slopes of Shiyane Hill provide a more spectacular setting for the subsequent clash with the Zulus – which did not happen at this point in the actual campaign – than the rather flat and featureless Zululand bank.

The two principal buildings that featured in the fighting of 1879 were demolished soon afterwards, but were rebuilt more or less on the original foundations in the 1880s. They give a very good impression of what their predecessors looked like, though there have been some changes, notably the

A few of these signs can be found on the flat ground between the post and the river at Rorke's Drift. They once held small interpretation notices, but these have suffered from water damage and most are no longer legible, though there are apparently plans to replace them. On the left of the picture can be seen the slopes of Shiyane with the mission buildings below.

replacement of the vulnerable thatched roofs with iron sheets. What was the hospital is now a museum and the storehouse further on is the mission church. Visitors are welcome to look inside the church, but must bear in mind that it is still a functioning place of worship and should be treated with appropriate respect. Outside the buildings rows of stones have been placed to mark the position of the British defensive works, making it easy to get an overview of the main features of the battlefield.

The road sign to Rorke's Drift on the approach from Elandskraal.

The entrance to the Rorke's Drift site, marked 'Shiyane Rorke's Drift', off the road between Dundee and Elandskraal. The white building on the left is the ELC Art and Craft centre. The car park is behind it to the left.

The best place to start a tour is probably in the south-western corner, closest to the road, where the first Zulu attack was directed. Modern buildings obscure part of the view, but it is still obvious that this part of the perimeter was extremely vulnerable. The shoulder of Shiyane Hill would have concealed the attackers until their final approach, while even closer to the defences the ground falls away steeply, providing an area of dead ground within 100 paces where the Zulus could rally. The visitor may wonder why

The ELC Art and Craft centre. This is a new building situated on the right as you enter the site, which contains a craft shop, café and toilets.

A good view of Shiyane Hill from the south can be obtained from the track leading to Rorke's Drift Lodge on the opposite side of the road. The track itself is a right of way, but on either side is private land and visitors should keep to the route at all times. What appears to be the summit of the hill when looking from Rorke's Drift is visible at far left, but from here it can be seen that the true summit is considerably further away.

Looking from the rear of the museum building towards the church. To the right of the church in 1879 was a small cookhouse, but this was left outside the defended perimeter.

Prince Dabulamanzi did not continue to attack in this sector instead of switching to the 'front' of the position. However, it should be borne in mind that the frontage here was far too narrow for the full strength of the Zulu Army to deploy, and that what is now the car park was then overgrown with scrub and trees and traversed by a low stone wall, making the approach less exposed than it would be today.

The path leading from the car park (on the right) towards the mission buildings, looking south-west in the direction of the site entrance. Today the site is very well maintained and easily accessible.

The first of the two main buildings that you will come to is the hospital/ museum. On the veranda outside is a three-dimensional model that depicts the terrain of the entire battlefield of 21–22 January 1879, from the ford on the Buffalo River to Isandlwana and beyond as far as Siphezi Mountain. Several points are especially worth noting. One is the relative sizes and positions of the two hills that feature so prominently in the story – Shiyane and Isandlwana. The former is considerably bigger, but has always attracted less attention because of its less spectacular profile. (In isiZulu Shiyane means 'eyebrow', alluding to the way in which the slopes appear to overhang the river.) The display also shows the steep and difficult nature of the country further down the Buffalo River beyond Fugitives' Drift. It will be remembered that Lord Chelmsford sent Major Bengough and his NNC column to patrol this route on the right flank of the main army, despite the unsuitability of the terrain for rapid movement and the lack of any realistic threat from that direction. A parallel route on the left flank can easily be traced out on the model, which would not only have involved better going, but might have intercepted the main Zulu *impi* on its way to its forming up positions on the Nqutu Plateau. Finally, the diorama sheds light on the question we asked at Isandlwana – how could the Zulu Army have moved from its position to the east of Isandlwana Hill to one behind the ridge to the north without being spotted by the British troops in the plain? It can be seen here that, although the terrain looks flat on the ground, it actually slopes gently downwards to the north-east, creating a large area of dead ground of which the soldiers in the camp would not have been aware.

Inside the museum you can follow the signs through a series of rooms with displays illustrating various aspects of the campaign and the battle itself. Apart from contemporary artefacts there are life-sized models of the combatants, and a diorama with thousands of miniature figures depicting the climax of the battle. It is easy to see from this how crowded the battlefield must have been with so many men crammed into this tiny area. Also of interest are some exposed sections of the original foundations that have been excavated by archaeologists. The internal arrangement of this building is not the same as that of the original hospital, but the maze of small rooms does give an idea of how claustrophobic it must have been for the defenders and patients trapped inside.

Outside the museum, the rock 'step' which used to run along the north-western side of the perimeter in front of the buildings has been partially obscured by graded earth ramps for easier access, but in a couple of places it can still be seen in its original condition. It is instructive to stand at the bottom of the step and imagine the predicament of a Zulu tasked with climbing it. Even without the mealie bags on the top – not to mention a line of redcoats with fixed bayonets – the feature is approximately man height, and would be a significant obstacle to scramble over. Colour Sergeant Bourne, in his 1936 reminiscences, remarked that the Zulus had not lived up to their reputation for cunning on this occasion, as they could have slit the mealie bags from below with their assegais and let the contents run out down the slope. No doubt from Bourne's position above this looked like a potential risk. The visitor looking at the site from a Zulu perspective, however, might feel emboldened to disagree. Even partially collapsed mealie bags, when

Looking towards Shiyane and the rocky terrace from the rear of the British perimeter. The path leading up the hill is reached via the gap in the trees at centre right.

The signpost to Jim Rorke's grave, behind the church.

added to the height of the natural step, would have been a sufficient obstacle, while large amounts of spilled grain underfoot would not have made the approach any easier.

Towards the north-eastern end of the site, lines of stones mark out the positions of the mealie bag barricade in front of the storehouse/church, and the transverse line of biscuit boxes linking this to the building itself. In the middle of the cramped space enclosed by these features is a surprisingly small circle of stones that indicates where the mealie bag redoubt was sited.

North-east of this, the 'well-built' stone cattle *kraal* has been reconstructed in roughly its original form. This was the end of the British position, and the spot where the final Zulu charges were made after dark on 22 January.

The British dead are buried in a small walled cemetery on the Shiyane side of the site, marked by a stone memorial engraved with their names. The carving was done soon after the battle by Private Melsop of C Company,

The grave of Jim Rorke, the original founder of the post, is reached by a path at the far end of the site. Rorke is said to have asked to be buried under these heavy slabs to prevent people or animals digging up his body.

who had been a stonemason in civilian life. There is a well-known story that he lacked the proper tools and had to use his bayonet for the job, but the obviously high quality of the work makes this seem unlikely. The Zulu casualties were interred in three mass graves, but these are outside the official battlefield site, on land belonging to the church, which at present does not encourage access. There are two monuments to the Zulu dead at the south-western end of the site. The oldest consists of a small stone pillar above a

The view northwards across the river from the site of Rorke's grave.

plaque bearing an inscription in English, isiZulu and Afrikaans. The new memorial, situated behind the craft centre, takes the form of a leopard lying on a pile of shields, with a symbolic buffalo thorn tree nearby.

A sign behind the church points to the grave of Jim Rorke, the founder of the original post, who is buried at the far end of the site overlooking the Buffalo River. In the Zulu language the place was also named after him – 'kwaJimu', or 'Jim's place'. Rorke died in 1875, allegedly as a result of his addiction to gin. It is said that when a shipment of his favourite drink went astray he was so upset that he committed suicide. By 1879 the site had come into the possession of the Swedish missionary, Otto Witt, from whom the British Army commandeered it as a supply base. It is one of the ironies of history that although Rorke did not even take part in the battle, its subsequent fame has made his name better known than those of many senior officers of the time.

JANET WELLS: A MISUNDERSTOOD RORKE'S DRIFT HEROINE?

One of the people who served at Rorke's Drift during the course of 1879, but who is not commemorated on the site, was Sister Janet Wells, who was transferred there after the end of hostilities from the military hospital at Utrecht. Already a veteran of the Russo-Turkish War of 1877–78, Nurse Wells is generally said to have been only 19 years old at the time. However, despite her youth and inexperience she forced through improvements in nursing care and sanitation, and dramatically reduced the death rate among the patients remaining at the post. She later treated both British and Zulu casualties of several battles, then moved to Cape Town where she met the captured King Cetshwayo. On returning to England in time for her twentieth birthday she became the second ever recipient of the Royal Red Cross for Nursing, the first being Florence Nightingale.

However, this inspiring story is not entirely accurate. The 1881 UK census shows her still living at home with her parents, but gives her age as 27. That this is not just a mistake is confirmed by the 1901 census, in which she is listed (under her married name of King) as 46. She was therefore approximately five years older at the time of the Anglo-Zulu War than is usually supposed – a fact that, while it does not detract in any way from her achievement, does help to make it more comprehensible. A biography of Janet Wells, *Sister Janet Nurse and Heroine of the Anglo-Zulu War 1879* by B. Best and K. Slossel, was published in 2004 by Pen & Sword.

Climbing Shiyane

Most visitors to Rorke's Drift confine themselves to the actual battle site around the mission buildings, but if you have the time the walk to the summit of Shiyane – the hill known to the British at the time as the Oskarberg – is highly recommended. It can be climbed in around 30 minutes, but you should allow 2 hours for a leisurely visit with time to admire the views. Don't forget to take plenty to drink, especially on a hot day. You will need to be back before 4 p.m. as the battle site closes then. A metal gate at the rear of the site leads to a track that climbs up the hill as far as a prominent rock shelf, beneath which are the caves where the Zulu marksmen had their firing positions. Here you can climb on to the shelf and look back towards the mission buildings. The distance is between 350 and 400 paces and it is hard to believe that the fire of the old smoothbore muskets and muzzle-loading rifles with which the Zulus were equipped was very effective at that range. On the other hand, the caves are easily seen from below, and would have been well within the effective range of the British Martini Henry. In a prominent position on top of the step is the mission bell. This marks the spot where Prince Dabulamanzi is said to have stood to direct the battle, though a position further up the hill would have commanded just as good a view while being less exposed to British fire.

Beyond the shelf the clearly marked track soon disappears. To avoid having to negotiate a series of barbed-wire fences you should turn right when you reach the first one, just below a group of houses. Do not go through the gate in the fence here. Continue to the right until just before you reach another house, then turn left and go straight uphill. You will soon come to another track running at right angles to your path around the hill; do not follow this but continue to climb. The walking is not difficult, but from here onwards there is no marked track and the going is not suitable for those with mobility issues. It is sometimes necessary to jump from rock to rock or duck under

Relatively few visitors make it to the top of Shiyane Hill, but the view from the top is well worth the effort.

A close-up view of one of the caves on Shiyane. These caves can be easily seen from the track leading up the hill, but exploring them is not advisable because of the presence of snakes and scorpions.

thorn bushes, and it would be wise to keep a lookout for snakes. There are good views back across the Buffalo River until you reach the summit ridge, but the actual summit is not visible from the Rorke's Drift site. In fact, the ridge that appears to be the summit when looking from below is less than halfway to the highest point. This is marked by a trig point at the far end of the ridge and commands spectacular views, especially to the north, east and south. The Reverend Smith and his party must have climbed to the area

Typical terrain on the upper slopes of Shiyane Hill. Thorns, spines and the occasional loose rock are the most obvious hazards, but the visitor should also keep a look out for snakes.

of the trig point in order to be able to see the activity around Isandlwana, and it is obvious from here that we must abandon any idea of them racing breathlessly down the final slope to alert the garrison to the approach of the Zulus; they would have had half a mile of scrambling across broken ground ahead of them before they even came in sight of the mission.

Unfortunately the summit is a popular picnic spot and tends to be littered with discarded plastic bottles and other rubbish – a situation that will only

175

Top: Looking north-west, upstream from Shiyane along the valley of the Buffalo River. The modern bridge at Rorke's Drift is in the middle distance.

Above: From the same point, the view to the east takes in the gorge of the Buffalo River between Rorke's and Fugitives' Drifts as well as the Batshe Valley, the scene of the first engagement of the war, in the distance.

get worse if a planned access road is built. There are also some ancient rock paintings on Shiyane, attributed to the San or Bushmen who inhabited the area many hundreds of years ago. No one knows how old the paintings are, but they have suffered badly from age and vandalism, and would be difficult to find without a local guide. A better place to see examples of San rock art is the Talana Museum in Dundee (overleaf).

The steep slope of Shiyane overlooking the river, looking towards the north.

THE TALANA MUSEUM

Talana House in the grounds of the Talana Museum, Dundee. This is the building where the exhibits on the Anglo-Zulu and Anglo-Boer Wars are housed.

There are good museums at both Isandlwana and Rorke's Drift, but the most comprehensive collection of Zulu War memorabilia is at the Talana Museum on the outskirts of Dundee (info@talana.co.za, Curator Pam MacFadden). The site is on the right as you approach the town from Nqutu; the car park is at the far end of the site, near the visitor centre from which you obtain your tickets. There is also a very good café here. At present the entrance fee is a very reasonable R25. The various buildings scattered around the site house a wide variety of displays illustrating aspects of daily life and industry in Natal, as well as the participation of its people in the wars of the late nineteenth and early twentieth centuries. Dundee was once a major coal mining area, and the region has since become famous for its glassware, which is featured in the main building. The Anglo-Zulu and Anglo-Boer War collections are in Talana House, behind the small rose garden on your left as you go up the road towards the car park. The museum suffered a burglary in October 2015 in which a number of very valuable medals from both wars were taken, but the rest of the collection was not affected. What makes the site of additional interest to military buffs is that

The cairn marking the spot where General Penn Symons was fatally wounded at the Battle of Talana in 1899. As a captain Symons had served in the 2nd/24th Foot in the Isandlwana campaign.

Looking north-eastwards from the site of General Penn Symons' memorial at Talana. While leading his men from the front, the general was shot by Boers firing from the surrounding hills.

it is actually on the spot where the first encounter of the Second Anglo-Boer War, the Battle of Talana, was fought in October 1899. Talana House was a British dressing station during the battle, and the nearby gum tree plantation was used by the British infantry for cover. Behind the house a path leads to a cairn that marks the spot where their commanding officer, Major General William Penn Symons, was fatally wounded by Boer fire from the hill on the right. (As Captain Penn Symons, incidentally, he had commanded D Company 2nd 24th Foot in the 1879 campaign, but was with Lord Chelmsford's column when the camp at Isandlwana was attacked. He was one of the advance party that relieved the defenders of Rorke's Drift on 23 January 1879.)

OTHER NEARBY SITES

At Rorke's Drift you are in the heart of the region of northern Kwazulu-Natal that has become known as 'The Battlefields'. During the nineteenth century this was the 'cockpit of Africa', and there are said to be around eighty sites here where British, Boers and Zulus clashed in the various wars. Not all are well signposted, or have much to see when you get there, so if you want to cover the area properly you would do best to join an organised tour or employ a guide, but most of the following sites can be visited independently.

Blood River (also known by its Zulu name of Ncome) is signposted off the R33 between Dundee and Vryheid, and from the R68 between Dundee and Nqutu. Andries Pretorius' Boers laagered their wagons along the banks of the river here in December 1838 and beat off an estimated 10,000 Zulus while suffering almost no casualties themselves. This apparent sign of God's favour made the site almost sacred to the Afrikaners of Boer descent, who have commemorated the victory with an extraordinary monument of sixty-four life-sized bronze wagons. There is now also a museum that attempts to provide a much-needed Zulu perspective on events.

Hlobane is about 20km from Vryheid. It is possible to walk across the plateau and descend via the notorious Devil's Pass, but the mountain is private property and is only accessible on an organised tour with a qualified guide.

Gingindlovu and Eshowe can be reached via the N2 north of Durban. There is not much to see at the battlefields themselves unless you have a good guide to explain the events, but Fort Nongqayi at Eshowe houses the Zululand Historical Museum, which is well worth a visit if you are in the area.

The minor road leading east from Ulundi towards the Hluhluwe-Imfolozi Game Reserve passes the Battle of Ulundi Memorial just outside the town. The park here is on the site where the British square halted to repulse the Zulu attack.

Majuba Hill, where the Boers defeated the British in 1881, is in the far north-western corner of Natal, off the N11 north of Newcastle. It is about 5km west of the road and is reached via a turning south of Charlestown. The mountain is often covered by low cloud and the climb to the top is steep, so a guide is recommended.

Ladysmith is easily reached via the N3 and N11 north-west of Pietermaritzburg, and unlike most of the battlefields it is accessible by public transport, as long distance coaches stop there on the Durban–Johannesburg route. The siege of Ladysmith by the Boers from October 1899 to February 1900 is commemorated in the Siege Museum in the centre of town.

The site of the Battle of Elandslaagte is signposted off the N11 about 26km north of Ladysmith. Colenso, where the Boers defeated a British attack on 15 December 1899, is 20km south of Ladysmith on the R203. The defeated British commander at Colenso was General Sir Redvers

This line of eucalyptus trees has been preserved to mark the position of the British firing line at Talana. Eucalyptus are ubiquitous in Natal nowadays, but are not native and would not have been present in Zululand in 1879.

Buller, whose misfortune at the hands of the Zulus at Hlobane has already been noted.

Near Chievely, 40km south of Ladysmith off the R103 to Estcourt, is the place where the Boers derailed an armoured train on 15 November 1899, capturing the young Winston Churchill among others. The spot is marked with a plaque but there is not much else to see here.

Spioenkop Nature Reserve, off the R600 38km west of Ladysmith, was the scene of the Battle of Spion Kop, fought between the British and the Boers in January 1900. There are signposted walking trails and interpretation signs. Spioenkop means 'spy hill', and the spectacular view from the top explains its importance as a military objective. The British, still led by the ill-fated Buller, captured the hill but were driven off it by Louis Botha's men with heavy losses.

A local guide who specialises in the First Anglo-Boer War and the 'minor battles' of the Anglo-Zulu War is Sean Friend (5 Uil Street, PO Box 2683, Newcastle, 2940, South Africa; seanfriend@telkomsa.net), who is the man to contact if you are interested in the battlefields at Hlobane, Khambula, Intombe Drift and Majuba. He also does highly recommended tours of Isandlwana and Rorke's Drift.

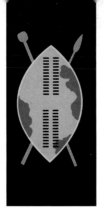

Recommended Reading

A great deal has been published about the Anglo-Zulu War and the battles of Isandlwana and Rorke's Drift in particular, and it is not easy to provide a brief reading list. The works mentioned below are just a few of the more recent ones that have been found particularly useful; most contain good bibliographies that will point the way to sources for further study.

I would start with Ian Knight's two Osprey Campaign Series books, *Rorke's Drift 1879: 'Pinned Like Rat in a Hole'* (1996) and *Isandlwana 1879: The Great Zulu Victory* (2002). Both give a brief overview of events, with a collection of illustrations and some good detailed maps. Each also has a short section on the battlefield today, though these are inevitably now rather dated. Ian Knight has an enormous amount of knowledge on all aspects of the Anglo-Zulu War, and several of his other works on the subject are listed here.

The late David Rattray's audio book, *The Day of the Dead Moon*, describes the background to the war and the events of both battles in his inimitable narrative style. The set of five CDs is available from Fugitives' Drift Lodge.

Rorke's Drift (London: Cassell, 2002) and *Isandlwana: How the Zulus Humbled the British Empire* (Barnsley: Pen & Sword, 2011) by Adrian Greaves together provide a thorough account of the events of 22 and 23 January from a professional historian who draws on a wealth of little-known sources.

Lieutenant Colonel Mike Snook's two volumes, *How Can Man Die Better* and *Like Wolves on the Fold,* (both Barnsley: Pen & Sword, 2010) deal with Isandlwana and Rorke's Drift respectively, though there is a great deal of overlap and in fact they are best read as two complementary volumes. Both are very well written by an experienced army officer whose professional viewpoint sheds much light on controversial aspects of the battles, though partly because of this it is easy to forget that much of the author's reconstructions of events remains speculative.

Several guidebooks to the battlefields have been published, of which the majority are now somewhat out of date, but the following are among those I have found useful:

Ian Knight's *The Zulu War Then and Now* (Oxford: Osprey Publishing, 1993) remains an invaluable guide to the appearance of the battlefields at the time of the war, though it is now more than 20 years old. It is a fascinating exercise to compare the views in old photographs to the same locations today, but this is a large and heavy volume not really suited to carrying around on a hot day.

Ian Castle and Ian Knight have written informative guidebooks to Rorke's Drift and Isandlwana in the 'Battleground South Africa' series, published by Leo Cooper in 2000 and 2001 respectively.

More recently, *The 24th Regiment, Isandlwana and Rorke's Drift* by Lieutenant Colonel Ian R. Gumm (In The Footsteps Battlefield Tours, Ross-on-Wye, 2015) combines a good account of the battles with details of a self-guided tour of the area, for which you would need your own car.

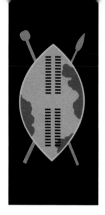

Bibliography

Among the thousands of publications on the Anglo–Zulu War, and the battles of Isandlwana and Rorke's Drift in particular, the general reader may find the following among the most useful and accessible. Also included here are a few works mentioned in the text that deal with less well-known aspects of the subject.

Bancroft, J.W. *Rorke's Drift: the Anglo-Zulu War 1879* (Stroud: Spellmount Publishers Ltd, 2004)

Best B. & Slossel, K. *Sister Janet: Nurse and Heroine of the Anglo-Zulu War 1879* (Barnsley: Pen & Sword, 2004)

Dodds, G.L. *The Zulus and Matabele: Warrior Nations* (London: Weidenfeld & Nicolson, 1998)

Golan, D. *Inventing Shaka: Using History in the Construction of Zulu Nationalism* (Boulder, Colorado: Lynne Rienner Publishers, 1994)

Guy. J. *The Destruction of the Zulu Kingdom: The Civil War in Zululand 1879–1884* (Pietermaritzburg, South Africa: University of Natal Press, 1994)

Knight, I. *Companion to the Anglo-Zulu War* (Barnsley: Pen & Sword, 2008)

Knight, I. *The Anatomy of the Zulu Army* (London: Greenhill Books, 1995)

Laband, J.P. *The Rise and Fall of the Zulu Nation* (London: Weidenfeld & Nicolson, 1997)

BIBLIOGRAPHY

Lock R. & Quantrill, P. *Zulu Victory: The Epic of Isandlwana and the Cover-up* (London: Greenhill Books, 2002)

Morris, D.R. *The Washing of the Spears* (London: Jonathan Cape, 1966)

Peers, C. *The African Wars: Warriors and Soldiers of the Colonial Campaigns* (Barnsley: Pen & Sword, 2010)

Raby, P. *Zulu: the Truth behind the Film* (York: Paul Raby, 2009)

Rattray, D. *A Soldier-Artist in Zululand — William Whitelock Lloyd and the Anglo-Zulu War of 1879* (Rorke's Drift, South Africa: Rattray Publications, 2007)

Thompson, P.S. *The Natal Native Contingent in the Anglo-Zulu War* (Scottsville, South Africa: Privately published, 2003)

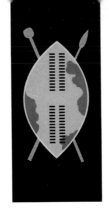

Index

INDEX

You may also be interested in …

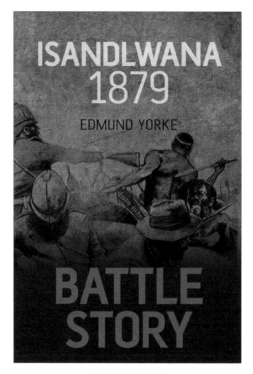

9780 7524 6201 1

Battle Story: Isandlwana 1879 explores
one of the most iconic battles in British
imperial and military history.

'Those well read in the history of the Zulu
War will find this book worthwhile, and
it would make an excellent introduction
for the novice.' – *The NYMAS Review*